The Total Enemy

POSTMODERN ETHICS SERIES

Postmodernism and deconstruction are usually associated with a destruction of ethical values. The volumes in the Postmodern Ethics series demonstrate that such views are mistaken because they ignore the religious element that is at the heart of existential-postmodern philosophy. This series aims to provide a space for thinking about questions of ethics in our times. When many voices are speaking together from unlimited perspectives within the postmodern labyrinth, what sort of ethics can there be for those who believe there is a way through the dark night of technology and nihilism beyond exclusively humanistic offerings? The series invites any careful exploration of the postmodern and the ethical.

Series Editors:

Marko Zlomislić (Conestoga College)
David Goicoechea (Brock University)

Other Volumes in the Series:

Cross and Khôra: Deconstruction and Christianity in the Work of John D. Caputo edited by Neal DeRoo and Marko Zlomislić

Agape and Personhood with Kierkegaard, Mother, and Paul (A Logic of Reconciliation from the Shamans to Today) by David Goicoechea

The Poverty of Radical Orthodoxy edited by Lisa Isherwood and Marko Zlomislić

Theologies of Liberation in Palestine-Israel: Indigenous, Contextual, and Postcolonial Perspectives edited by Nur Masalha and Lisa Isherwood

Agape and the Four Loves with Nietzsche, Father, and Q (A Physiology of Reconciliation from the Greeks to Today) by David Goicoechea

Fundamentalism and Gender: Scripture—Body—Community edited by Ulrike Auga, Christina von Braun, Claudia Bruns, and Jana Husmann

The Total Enemy

Six Chapters of a Violent Idea

MIKKEL THORUP

POSTMODERN ETHICS SERIES 8

PICKWICK *Publications* · Eugene, Oregon

THE TOTAL ENEMY
Six Chapters of a Violent Idea

Postmodern Ethics 8

Pickwick Publications
An Imprint of Wipf and Stock Publishers
199 W. 8th Ave., Suite 3
Eugene, OR 97401

www.wipfandstock.com

ISBN 13: 978-1-62564-898-3

Cataloguing-in-Publication Data

Thorup, Mikkel

The total enemy : six chapters of a violent idea / Mikkel Thorup.

xvi + 156 p. ; 23 cm. Includes bibliographical references.

ISBN 13: 978-1-62564-898-3

1. Terror. 2. Terrorism—Case Studies. 3. Violence—Case Studies. 4. Enemies. I. Title. II. Series.

HV6431 T575 2015

Manufactured in the U.S.A.   02/23/2015

Contents

Acknowledgments

ONE CAN BE UNEXPECTEDLY hit by enmity by walking down the street, minding one's own business only to suddenly be called a "faggot," "slut," "nigger," etc. Enmity is rarely a mutual affair. Often it is forced upon us by someone we did not know or did not consider our enemy. The enmification does tend to create what it names, namely a relation of enmity, if for no other reason than that of self-defense. Acts of enmity often appear out of the blue creating proper enemies.

However, so does acts of kindness and friendship. They too come unsolicited and unexpected. And this is how this book came about. I had published chapter 4 on a website and received shortly thereafter an email from a man unknown to me telling me he liked the piece and would I consider turning it into a book. The kindness of a stranger came from Professor Mark Zlomislic who not only encouraged me to expand the article into a book but also offered a book series edited by him in which to do it. I am very grateful to Mark for not only reaching out, calling me a friend in the academic community, but also offering his help, even when I turned his suggestion into something quite different than his initial proposal. This is truly an act of friendship for which I thank him and hope to be able to reciprocate.

The chapters in this book have all been written separately and published in various places and can, in that sense, stand alone. They do, however, all reflect on the same basic question, which is, I think, the one that triggered Mark's interest to begin with, namely the relation between modernity and its empowerment of humankind's capacities for history making, on the one hand, and then political violence and enmity, on the other hand. That has been my main interest since writing a PhD dissertation called "In Defence of Enmity" (2003–5), investigating Enlightenment liberalism as well as what I call liberal globalism and their relations to violence and enmity. I also investigated the theme in An Intellectual History of Terror (2010) as well as a number of books in Danish on totalitarianism, anti-terrorism, piracy, counter-enlightenment, contemporary security debates, and most explicitly in a small, popular volume simply called Enmity (2013).

The case studies in this book reflect this ongoing interest and I would like to thank my colleagues and students at the Department of Intellectual History at the University of Aarhus for listening to me going on and on about these issues year after year. I strongly believe that all worthwhile thinking is done aloud and in the company of interested people, strangers, or intimates, and I hope all the comments and critiques that I have received over the years are adequately reflected in the chapters that follow hereinafter. They are, in any case, greatly appreciated.

Introduction

ON MARCH THE 3RD 1937 Joseph Stalin gave a speech to the plenum of the Central Committee of the Russian Communist Party.[1] In the speech he accused his fellow party members of insufficient awareness and vigilance towards what he calls "the wrecking and diversionist-espionage work of agents of foreign countries." These agents are predominantly but not exclusively Trotskyists and Stalin wants to remind his audience that the wonderful progress of the Soviet state has not diminished but rather augmented the enemy challenge. He quotes a confidential letter from the Central Committee: "We must remember that the more hopeless the position of the enemies become, the more readily they will clutch at extreme measures as the only measures of the doomed in their struggle against Soviet power." There are, Stalin says, no ends to enmity.

The enemy used to appear openly in what he calls a "political tendency." But the vigorous working class opposition and the successful Soviet state has forced the enemy to change tactics. Trotskyism "has transformed into a frenzied and unprincipled band of wreckers, diversionists, spies and killers, acting upon the instructions of the intelligence service organs of foreign states." Trotskyism is now a full-blown treasonous but also hidden force. Is this, Stalin wonders aloud, why party members have failed to be vigilant and why "at times they themselves assisted in promoting agents of foreign states to responsible posts?" How are we, he asks what must have been a frightened audience eager to applaud and show signs of enthusiastic support, "to explain that our Party comrades, despite their experience in the struggle against anti-Soviet elements, despite the numerous warning signals and precautionary signs, proved to be politically short-sighted in

---

1. Stalin, "Defects in Party Work."

the face of the wrecking, espionage-diversionist work of the enemies of the people?"

Stalin's enemy transformed from a clear, identifiable political opponent to a hidden -ism and he has completely decoupled success from peace, party membership from loyalty, visibility from existence, appearance from reality, and established an enemy so frightful in its work and its stealth that no other measure is appropriate than an all-out war turned inwards at the people who believe themselves loyal party members. All members are in effect asked to hunt, identify and name the hidden enemy or see themselves accused of fault by either complicity, active as treason or inactive as carelessness. The enemy is everywhere and one becomes one oneself by inattention to that fact which are hidden from sight but now proclaimed by Stalin. War is normality, peace is surrender.

Stalin's speech is a remarkable documentation of the 'total enemy'-thinking. The total enemy is the one whose identity and deeds are substituted for analogies and being; whose sole purpose in life is destruction and violence; who is present even when not apparent; and with whom no co-existence will ever be possible because the total enemy will never let go, never allow peace and prosperity to become the order of the day. The war against the total enemy is therefore eternal. It must ultimately turn inward and is always associated very strongly with notions of betrayal, inner enemies and hidden, degenerative forces masquerading as friends.

There is an inner tension in Stalin's speech: Victory is inevitable, but eternally postponed. The total enemy is what comes in between victory as inevitable and victory as reality. Violence becomes the necessary means to narrow the gap between inevitability, without which the whole Soviet edifice implodes, and reality. Violence is the history-making force and the total enemy is the field of applied history-making violence.

Modernity and violence

Violence speaks in the form of hurting and screaming, but it also speaks of its own righteousness. This is at least the case with political violence. In modernity, political violence must speak. Modern violence has to legitimize itself—a legitimization that has a history. Modernity here means the period from the mid-eighteenth century to the present—the age of modern politics.

In trying to legitimate an action, you are never completely detached from your surroundings; this is even the case when someone attacks those surroundings. By using violence, one is often at a disadvantage in terms of legitimation; one has to redescribe what is perhaps universally thought of as horrendous as being actually benign and moral. This can only be done by drawing on already established criteria of 'the good'.

In relation to violence, one has to capitalize on the authority of the available languages of legitimacy. One has to appeal to the sensibilities of one's audience and speak within the established parameters of categories of morality. The degrees of freedom when trying to convince an audience is determined by the languages already present. This is why Quentin Skinner argues that,

> [all revolutionaries] are obliged to march backwards into battle. To legitimise their conduct, they are committed to showing that it can be described in such a way that those who currently disapprove of it can be brought to see that they ought to withhold their disapproval of it. To achieve this end, they have no option but to show that at least some of the terms used by their ideological opponents to describe what they admire can be applied to include and thus to legitimise their own seemingly questionable behaviour.[2]

In *The Civilizing Process* Norbert Elias writes the following about pre-modern view on violence:

> Outbursts of cruelty did not exclude one from social life. They were not outlawed. The pleasure in killing and torturing others was great, and it was a socially permitted pleasure. To a certain extent, the social structure even pushed its members in this direction, making it seem necessary and practically advantageous to behave in this way.[3]

Elias fails to recognize the warrior ethos as a legitimization of violence. However, he does highlight a difference between the pre-modern and modern relation to violence. In pre-modern Europe, violence was predominantly viewed as an integral part of everyday life. Violence was more prevalent than today. Violence was considered an inescapable part of life. No act, excepting perhaps the second coming, could change the constancy

---

2. Skinner, "Moral Principles and Social Change," 150.
3. Elias, *The Civilizing Process*, 163.

and presence of violence. Violence needed no explanation. It was destiny, and an integral part of the human condition. Modernity changes this:

> Cruelty as entertainment, human sacrifice to indulge superstition, slavery as a labor-saving device, conquest as the mission statement of government, genocide as a means of acquiring real estate, torture and mutilation as routine punishment, the death penalty for misdemeanors and differences of opinion, assassination as the mechanism of political succession, rape as the spoils of war, pogroms as outlets for frustration, homicide as the major form of conflict resolution—all were unexceptionable features of life for most of human history. But today, they are rare to nonexistent in the West, far less common elsewhere than they used to be, concealed when they do occur, and widely condemned when they are brought to light.[4]

The modern imperative surrounding violence is what Hans Joas aptly calls "the dream of a modernity without violence."[5] When violence becomes a product of humankind, an accidental or non-necessary part of life, its continuance also becomes a scandal. Violence is now a quality not of nature but of society and its institutions. One can no longer (as easily) refer to the violent nature of the world as justification of one's own violence. Violent narratives have to include a promise to abolish, minimize, or prevent violence. Violence now has to justify itself as anti-violence.

What is a total enemy?

Basically, the enemy is someone willfully standing in the way of realizing one's most important goals; the one who is actively hindering happiness. The enemy is always an attacker. There has to be an active element, an evil intention, on the part of the enemy, making his or her actions, or even being, directed at the other's person, life, desires, etc. As a slogan for the TV-series Last Resort said, "The enemy is the one keeping you from getting home." The enemy is the one I have to fight in order to live my life in a way that is content and secure.

Enmities come in banal and catastrophic forms, from neighbor quarrels to genocides. They come in all shapes and with all kinds of consequences. A brief history of enmity would—following Reinhart Koselleck's

4. Pinker, "A History of Violence."
5. Joas, *War and Modernity*, chapter 1.

notion of asymmetrical counter-concepts[6]—suggest that European history has witnessed a number of shifts in enmity starting with the antique duality between stasis, an unnatural civil war among brother peoples, among Greeks, and then polemós, a natural and perpetual enmity between Greeks and non-Greeks. This dual concept of enmity was then first developed by the Romans and then given a more dynamic form in the Christian Middle Ages with a distinction between an unnatural and regrettable enmity between Christian princes and peoples and then a natural enmity between Christians and heathens. This latter enmity was more dynamic because the enemy was in a position to convert and then change status, but it was probably also more violent exactly because of that because the enemy became the one who had been exposed to the truth but had renounced it. With the development of the great territorial states, the language of enmity shifted from theology to law and politics. The states took upon themselves the prerogative of naming the enemy. This is the era of the 'public enemy' where the enemy is not particular persons but the abstract persona of the state. Here, we have, as a core developmental principle of statehood, the notion of a non-discriminatory right to war. The statist enemy is not a heathen or a criminal—in theory, not so much in actual practice or language—but rather the opposing state will. Concurrently with this, we have the development of what became the colonial enmity directed at a non-acknowledged other. This viewpoint was summarized brutally by the American foreign minister Richard Olney in 1907 in an article celebrating international law among civilized peoples: "Savage tribes and scattered nomadic and casual collections of men may be disregarded," that is, they can have no legal rights to protection because they have no proper political form.[7]

The colonial enemy shares many features with the total enemy, not least its one-sidedness and brutality. The activation of the total enemy in totalitarianism borrowed heavily from colonial languages and practices but I would suggest that some internal factors were equally important of which I would highlight the relation between history making and violence as suggested in the paragraph hereinabove, a broadening of politics, and the ideas contained within the idea of 'the total' developed in the first decades of the 20th century.

When violence came in the service of non-violence, when it became a political instrument of history making, a new dynamic was unleashed for

6. Koselleck, "The Historical-Political."
7. Olney, "The Development of International Law," 421.

good and bad. The first chapters in this book explore some of the ways political actors used and developed the notion of political violence. Coupled with a notion of the enemy, which is then the epicenter of continued violence, which is violence personified, a violent potential is present. This is, I would suggest, modernity's double notion of violence: a self-description as non-violence, of non-violence in the making, and an identification of the causes and actors behind continued violence. This is what allows political actors to use violence in modernity, the externalization of its causes and the imperative to address that violence.

The modern concept of the enemy contained in the dualism between state enemies and colonial enemies was challenged from around the middle of the 19th century onwards, when 'the social', 'the people', and 'the population' emerged as categories in their own right. In relation to enmity their contribution was to broaden the sources of enmity and the entities in need of protection. Three paradigmatic, albeit quite different, expressions of this were socialism's emphasis of the social, nationalism's emphasis of the people, and racism's emphasis of the population. When these phenomena became political concepts and fields of action the statist control of enmity threatened to dissolve, but various state forms answered by incorporating these into new conceptualizations of the enemy, the totalitarian states most prominently and explicitly.

In the early decades of the 20th century, a new notion of politics was developed that was centered on the concept of the total. This is discussed in the mid-section of the book. It culminates in the totalitarian states of Germany, Italy, and Russia where 'the total', which is an idea of a complete politicization or rather stateification, is coupled with enmity into a new and frightening concept of the total enemy. Some of the most significant features of the total enemy are:

- an absolute opposition between friend and enemy. No competitors, only mortal enemies.

- no neutrality exists. Dissent is treason. Suspicion and paranoia are normality.

- the threat is existential. It concerns survival (of nation, race, God…).

- the threat is always both external and internal.

- war is the natural, eternal, and inevitable condition of humankind, individually and collectively.

- war is everything and everywhere.

- the threat is many-sided: military, social, biological, political, and criminal.

- the threat and the enmity is absolute. It is the first and last concern.

- continuous destruction of the enemy is the primary political practice. Total victory is needed but always postponed.

This way of thinking is chillingly summarized in the 1975-flag song of the Cambodian Khmer Rouge:

> Glittering red blood blankets the earth
> Sacrificial blood to liberate the people
> Blood of workers, peasants and intellectuals
> Blood of young men, Buddhist monks and young women
> Blood that swirls away and takes flight, twirling on high into the sky
> Turning into the red, revolutionary flag!
>
> Red flag! Red flag! Now floating on high! Now floating on high!
> O comrades, seethe with anger in order to destroy the enemy!
> Red flag! Red flag! Now floating on high! Now floating on high!
> Let our fury swoop down like a tornado!
> Don't spare a single reactionary, a single imperialist!
> Make a clean sweep of the Kampuchean soil!
> Seething with anger, let us move into the attack!
> Let us wipe out all enemies of Kampuchea!
> Let us grasp the Victory! The Victory! The Victory![8]

The wish to understand the thinking behind those song lines motivates this book. The guiding wish is to explore how that mode of enmity thought emerged historically and how it still structures much, arguably far too much, thought, and practice.

Structure of the book

The book consist of six case-studies, each exploring and discussing histori-cally specific expressions of depicting an enemy that the actors believe can only be dealt with using extreme violence.

The first part, Pre-histories of the total enemy, looks at two important sites in the development of the total enemy, the French Revolution, and

8. Locard, *Pol Pot's Little Red Book*, 40.

the emergence of terrorist thinking in the middle of the 19th century. The argument in this part is that a connection exists between the features of modernity and a more dynamic, but also dangerous, concept of the enemy as well as an idea of violence as a creative political force making societal change possible.

The middle part, State histories of the total enemy, deals with the 20th century, firstly with the pre-WWII conceptualizations of the 'total' in European political thought as an answer to a liberal state deemed unfit to manage and control mass society. This is where enmity and the total first come into contact, like in the concept of "total war" but where the main innovation is on the development of the total. The next chapter deals specifically with the totalitarian enemy in Nazi Germany especially but also Soviet Russia. It does so by looking at how observers and thinkers in Europe have tried to understand the dramatically new and intensified enmity of totalitarian states.

The third and final part, Private contemporary histories of the total enemy, investigates two forms of contemporary total enmity, in Islamism and in right-wing extremism and these chapters look specifically at what happens to the total enemy concept once it goes from a state concept in the 20th century to a private practice in the 21st century. By looking at Osama bin Laden and Anders Breivik, especially as representatives of two streams of total enmity today, the book considers how they narrate an enmification into being, closing with a discussion of what processes of total enmification we are up against at present.

I

Pre-Histories of the Total Enemy

1

Salutary Terror: Inventing the Concepts of Terror and Terrorism

"IT IS TIME," SAID a Jacobin delegation in 1793, "that equality bore its scythe above all heads. It is time to horrify all the conspirators. So legislators, place Terror on the order of the day! Let us be in revolution, because everywhere counter-revolution is being woven by our enemies. The blade of the law should hover over all the guilty."[1]

The French Revolution[2] inaugurates the age of revolutions. The American Revolution was the first modern revolution but it was the French that became the model and inspiration,[3] not least because the American Revolution was primarily a national liberation whereas the French Revolution was a political and social revolution. This is so not least because the French Revolution, which started as a classic petition to the king, turned into both a general denial of the past and its institutions as well as not merely a political revolt aimed at regime or ruler change but into a societal revolution remodeling French society and political language as such.[4] It basically turned from arguing on behalf of customary justice into developing a whole new conception of justice based on equality, starting what Alexis de Tocqueville

1. Andress, *The Terror*, 179.

2. Soboul, *The French Revolution 1787–1799*; Lefebvre, *The Coming of the French Revolution*; Kates, *The French Revolution*.

3. Arendt, *On Revolution*, 56.

4. Mayer, *The Furies*, chapter 1.

would later describe as a democratic revolution, a new understanding of justice based on "equality of conditions."[5] What was not just a revolution in fact but in language as well is the possibility hereafter to legitimize oneself by reference to the future, to the not-yet-there, the event-turning-into-fact, making 'old' into a term of abuse rather than a sign of noble truth. As Immanuel Wallerstein notes: "[I]n the political arena, modernity means the acceptance of the 'normality' of change, as opposed to its 'abnormality', its transitory character."[6]

What the French Revolution did was to provide proof for the possibility of change in an old, traditional country (unlike the young and therefore unique country of the United States). "If revolution could happen in France, then there was hardly a cranny or crevice of Europe that might not bear the revolutionary burden."[7] This also helps explain why revolutionary upheavals seem mostly to take place in countries experiencing an improvement in political or economic conditions. It shows that change is possible and only then does the forces of change gain momentum. This is incidentally also why all revolutionary groups narrate their struggle into other already successful struggles and why a process of radicalization can happen relatively fast as it did in the French Revolution which only became anti-monarchical well into the process.

The French Revolution signals a shift in the conceptual meaning of terror in two tempi. Firstly we have the "Robespierrean moment," giving the concept of terror a futuristic element, separating the concept from its unqualified meaning of fear and its quasi-political meaning of policing, ordinary or extraordinary, and merging it with ideas of virtue and creation. Secondly we have the "anti-Robespierrean moment" separating the concept from the (regular or legitimate) state and monopolizing it among illegitimate states (despotisms) and private actors (terrorists).

In clear contrast to contemporary usage the concept of terror is used by the Jacobins as a concept of order and creation of order. In his book *Holy Terror* Terry Eagleton writes that "terrorism began life as state terrorism. It was a violence visited by the state on its enemies, not a strike against sovereignty by its faceless foes."[8] The same is related by David C. Rapoport: "When the term [terror] entered our language in 1795, terrorism was seen

5. Tocqueville, *Democracy in America*, 3.

6. Wallerstein, *After Liberalism*, 233.

7. Leiden and Schmitt, *The Politics of Violence*, 11.

8. Eagleton, *Holy Terror*, 1.

as the indispensable tool to establish a democratic order."[9] As I have shown elsewhere[10] this is not altogether true but it captures very precisely the difference between the Robespierrean and the anti-Robespierrean usage.

The French Revolution 1: Robespierre

In 1789 the Jacobin Jean-Paul Marat, an active spokesman for revolutionary violence, advocated terror as the revolutionary approach to dealing with despotism. It was, according to Marat mobilizing the deterrent usage in a political context, the spontaneous violence of the street which had "bent the aristocratic faction of the Estates-General . . . by using terror to remind them of their duty."[11] This is a passive understanding of terror, making people refrain from doing something. But soon after, in his newspaper *Ami du Peuple* no. 35 from 1790, Marat coined a more active understanding of terror, of "a state of beneficial terror which is indispensable in accomplishing the great work of the constitution."[12] In *Journal de la République Francaise* from 23 January 1793 he writes: "The execution of Louis XVI, far from troubling the peace of the state, will only serve to strengthen it, not only by containing the internal enemies through terror, but also the external enemies."[13] The passive or perhaps rather directive understanding of terror could obviously be used for counter-revolutionary purposes as done in July 1792 by the king's foreign minister, the counter-revolutionary count Montmorin, who proposed to "strike the Parisians with terror" since "only fear pushes the Assembly in one direction until another terror pushes it in another"[14] thereby using the concept of terror in a defensive or restorative sense emphasizing its frightening and avenging qualities.

At the end of 1792 Robespierre said that any revolution have a period of armed struggle legitimated by its purpose but "as yet unsupported by just laws." The execution of Louis XVI should therefore proceed immediately "to nourish in the spirit of tyrants a salutary terror of the justice of the people" [la terreur salutaire de la justice du people] if not exactly of the

---

9. Rapoport, "The Fourth Wave," 419.

10. Thorup, *An Intellectual History of Terror*, chapter 5.

11. Mayer, *The Furies*, 101.

12. van den Heuvel, "Terreur, Terroriste, Terrorisme", 99.

13. Marat, "The Execution of the Tyrant."

14. Mayer, *The Furies*, 121 and 172.

laws.[15] This is a usage seemingly combining terror's deterrent meaning with a political purpose. A year later, on 21 November 1793, in an attack on the dechristianization campaign, he more explicitly used the deterrent and religious meaning when the referred to God as "a source of confidence to the virtuous and of terror to the criminal."[16]

On 30 August 1793 a Royer spoke in the Jacobin club about the need to make "terror the order of the day" [la terreur à l'ordre du jour][17] as the "only way to arouse the people and force them to save themselves."[18] He gives the concept a mobilizing significance and a few days later, on 5 September, terror was made official policy as a means to "organize, systematize and accelerate repression of the Republic's domestic adversaries."[19] This was a policy long argued for by for instance Jacques-Nicolas Billaud-Varenne who in the summer of 1794 signed more death warrants than Robespierre and who radicalized both the paranoia of the revolutionaries as well as their belief in the cleansing effects of terror.[20]

There was then an established although perhaps not dominant discourse of terror already present and active when Robespierre in his speech of 5 February 1794 about the principles of political morality says that democratic principles must inform the government:

> But in order to found democracy and consolidate it among us, in order to attain the peaceful reign of constitutional laws, we must complete the war of liberty against tyranny and weather successfully the tempests of the revolution; such is the aim of the revolutionary government that you have organized. You must therefore still regulate your conduct by the stormy circumstances in which the republic finds itself, and the plan of your administration should be the result of the spirit of the revolutionary government combined with the general principles of democracy.[21]

Robespierre makes a distinction between the normal state of affairs characterized by "the peaceful reign of constitutional laws" and then the present

15. Scurr, *Fatal Purity*, 223; Robespierre, "Opinion sur le jugement de Louis XVI," 130.

16. Scurr, *Fatal Purity*, 266.

17. Walther, "Terror, Terrorismus," 343.

18. Mayer, *The Furies*, 196.

19. Furet, "Terror," 137.

20. Burney, "The fear of the executive."

21. Robespierre, "Report on the Principles of Political Morality," 279.

exceptional or foundational state. At the moment of the speech it is simultaneously a situation of exception, with foreign and domestic enemies, and a revolutionary moment. Once the crisis is over, then firstly the exception and secondly the revolution can stop and give way to the institutionalization of everyday life making the state of exception into an institution rather than the moment of emergence and creation it is at the time of the speech.

Terror, then, becomes the tool of both the state of exception, which is not new as practice, and the state of revolution or creation which is something new altogether both as practice and concept. Robespierre continues with his most famous or infamous sentences:

> Externally all the despots surround you; internally all the friends of tyranny conspire; they will conspire until crime is deprived of all hope. It is necessary to annihilate both the internal and external enemies of the republic or perish with its fall. Now, in this situation your first political principle should be that one guides the people by reason, and the enemies of the people by terror [la terreur]. If the driving force of popular government in peacetime is virtue, that of popular government during a revolution is both virtue and terror: virtue, without which terror is destructive; terror, without which virtue is impotent. Terror is only justice that is prompt, severe, and inflexible; it is thus an emanation of virtue; it is less a distinct principle than a consequence of the general principle of democracy applied to the most pressing needs of the patrie.
>
> It has been said that terror is the spring of despotic government. Does yours, then, resemble despotism? Yes, as the swords that flash in the hands of the heroes of liberty resemble those with which the satellites of tyranny are armed. Let the despot govern his debased subjects by terror; he is right as a despot: conquer by terror the enemies of liberty and you will be right as founders of the republic. The government of the revolution is the despotism of liberty against tyranny. Is force only intended to protect crime? And is not the destiny of lightning to strike prideful heads?[22]

Virtue is here a republican citizen virtue emphasizing putting the nation above the personal, devotion to the common good, defense of liberty and sovereignty and the will to sacrifice oneself should the need arise. This kind of virtue is meant to set the benign terror apart from the personalized terror of the despot. The quotation is also in clear opposition to despotic drawn out torture and mutilation and its "privileges of death" which stipulated

---

22. Robespierre, "Report on the Principles of Political Morality," 273–74.

different punishments for different social classes. This is probably one of the reasons why Robespierre describes the workings of the righteous terror as 'justice that is prompt, severe, and inflexible'.

In May 1791 Dr. Guillotin had proposed his penal reform stating in its first paragraph: "Crimes of the same kind shall be punished by the same kind of punishment, whatever the rank of the criminal." The second paragraph proscribes decapitation "by means of a machine" for all capital punishments "whatever the crime" making the punishment equal and humanitarian by minimizing suffering (though not the public spectacle).[23] It is interesting to note that Robespierre at the discussion in the Assembly was against death penalty as such as well as against beheading.[24] Perhaps the new humanist guillotine was also a reaction to the lynch mobs at the time exploding into beheadings and mutilations, trying to direct the sans-culotte energies into the role of spectator rather than actor (Danton famously said in regard to the formation of the Revolutionary Tribunal: "Let us be terrible, so that the people does not have to be.").[25] Robespierre had shown understanding if not even approval of this kind of spontaneous revolutionary 'justice' when he said of the storming of the Bastille that "the terror inspired by this national army, ready to present itself in Versailles, determined the Revolution."[26] He seems to be saying that the terror of parading around Paris with the head of the Bastille commander and the city chief magistrate on pikes created a point of no return for the revolution.

His combination of terror and virtue as "a consequence of the general principle of democracy applied to the most pressing needs of the patrie" describes the protection of the republic in dangerous times, a new kind of egalitarian justice as well as terror as what we could call "gruesome humanism," doing what is necessary to defend the liberty gains, reminding oneself and others not to become soft in a mistaken humanism and then losing it all to the forces which will make terror not the exception but the norm. Righteous terror then becomes less cruel than humanist inaction because of the promise of justice and peace which it carries contrary to the promise

---

23. Kershaw, *A History of the Guillotine*; Fife, *The Terror,* ch. 3; Smith, *Punishment and Culture*, chapter 5.

24. Scurr, *Fatal Purity*, 133–36.

25. Andress, *The Terror*, 213.

26. Scurr, *Fatal Purity*, 85.

of continued repression and death which inaction and therefore counter-revolution and restoration promise.[27]

But there is obviously much more than that at stake. Robespierre could be said to use the regime typology from one his great inspirations, Montesquieu, combining the virtue of the republic with the terror of the temporary despotism. What made the combination possible was exactly the permanent virtue of the republic and the temporary despotism needed for the republic's survival, a "despotism of liberty against tyranny." But that is not all he does. He doesn't restrict his usage to the deplorable but necessary defensive violence; it does not center solely on a state of exception, but importantly also on a state of creation. Terror is at the time of the French Revolution already a word for the instrumental or deterrent qualities of state violence. This is not what Robespierre adds to the concept. He combines this usage with a progressive philosophy of history making terror into a creative force. Terror *as* justice was unknown until this period (known was terror in the service of justice). Robespierre draws upon the Enlightenment connection between terror and despotism saying that despotism is generalized terror but his novelty is making terror an instrument for politics: terror to achieve the termination of all violence and injustice. Terror is no longer just an instrument of police but now also of politics. Robespierre adds a positive feature to the concept. It is no longer, in its political sense, just a state concept of order, *defense* of the existing order (legitimate as police, illegitimate as despotism) but rather also a revolutionary concept of state or *order making*. Terror is in the state of exception what the dictatorship of the proletariat becomes for communism in the revolution: an instrument to preserve the order in the making, order coming into its own, hence its character as both protection and creation.

Thomas Thornton differentiates between "enforcement terror" perpetrated by those in power (anti-terror, state of exception, repression) and "agitational terror" perpetrated by those challenging power (terrorism, rebellion, revolution).[28] Robespierre's innovation is to combine those two at the exact moment that "agitational terror" came into being, that is, he is both one of the prime innovators of the idea that violence can serve to

---

27. Sutherland, *France 1789-1815*; Steiner, "Aspects of Counter-Revolution"; Boffa, "Counter-revolution"; Mayer, *The Furies*, chapter 2; Davies, *Extreme Right in* France, chapter 2; Brown, *Ending the French Revolution*.

28. Thornton, "Terror as a weapon of political agitation," 42.

bring about the absolute new while at the same time being primarily concerned to defend what has already emerged.

Louis de Saint-Just, friend and ally of Robespierre,[29] member of the Committee of Public Safety, a key player in the Parisian part of the reign of terror, and executed together with Robespierre said on 3 March 1794:

> let nothing evil be either pardoned or unpunished in the government, and justice will be more fearful to enemies of the Republic than terror alone. How many traitors have escaped a terror which merely talks who would not escape from a justice which weighs crimes in its hand! Justice condemns enemies of the people and partisans of tyranny among us to eternal slavery. Terror lets them hope for an end to it; for all tempests come to an end, and you have seen this; justice condemns civil servants to integrity; justice makes the people happy and consolidates the new order of things; terror is a two-edged weapon which some have used to avenge the people and others to serve tyranny; terror has filled the prisons, but the guilty are not punished; the terror has passed by like a thunderstorm. Do not look for lasting severity in the public character except from the strengths of institutions; a dreadful calm always follows our tempests, and we are also more indulgent after terror than before it.[30]

And he also made the connection between the revolution and terror clear by saying: "There are three sins against the republic: one is to be sorry for state prisoners; another is to be opposed to the rule of virtue; and the third is to be opposed to the terror."[31] Saint-Just has a quite instrumental view of terror. It is just violence: "[T]error is a double-edged sword: some use it to avenge the people, others to serve tyranny."[32] But, of course, the use of it "to avenge the people" makes it a violence very unlike that "to serve tyranny." There was then something of a consensus, or at the very least a discourse among the radicals, of terror as both a statist concept of order and as a revolutionary concept of creation.

What Robespierre and his allies do is politicizing the concept, that is, turning the concept from a description of what various actors and events

---

29. On the thinking of Robespierre and Saint-Just making a distinction between the "errors" of patriots and the "crimes" of counter-revolutionaries see Bates, *Enlightenment Aberrations*, chapter 6.

30. Saint-Just in Beik, *The French Revolution*, 295.

31. Scurr, *Fatal Purity*, 276.

32. Mayer, *The Furies*, 208.

caused of fear in the individual into a political concept about how this fear might help create the future. Terror is an instrument for bringing about a new society. Terror is not to be the defining quality of the new society, as the Enlightenment claimed about despotism or as the anti-Robespierreans claimed and claims about the Jacobins.[33] Terror is the instrument to come past terror in all its connotations, as everything avoidable which frightens or harms man. This is also why Saint-Just talks about letting institutions replace terror and Robespierre talks about the peaceful reign of constitutional laws. Revolutionary violence is illegitimate acts wanting to become legitimate, just as it is illegal violence wanting to become the new legality. Only success does that, all else is crime or terrorism.

Paradoxically, it may be because of the fall of Robespierre that the regime came to be known as the "Reign of Terror." It didn't succeed to emerge as a legitimate, consolidated order being able to count on the veil of silence which is bestowed on those who manage to become accepted as legitimate equals in the inter-state system. It remained "terroristic" because stopped in its tracks. The Jacobin violence was launched or rather accelerated with a slogan of making "terror the order of the day" and didn't manage or have time to become something else. Terror becomes therefore not, as Robespierre said it, a temporary instrument against the contra-revolutionary forces but a regime form.[34]

This acceleration of terror into a system is most evident in the infamous Law of 22 Prairial voted into effect on 10 June 1794. The law denied the accused the right to legal counsel; allowed the prosecution to introduce "moral proofs"; vastly accelerated the entire judicial process; jurors were to be handpicked by the Committee of Public Safety; sentencing was limited to the stark choice between acquittal and death; and its §6 expanded the concept of treason into just about everyone.[35] In the introduction to the law is stated very clearly the rationale behind revolutionary justice, mimicking the rhetoric described above and violently insisting upon and creating a clear distinction between friends and enemies:

> the crime of the conspirators directly threatens the existence of society or its liberty, which is the same thing. Here, the life of villains and the life of the people are pitted against one another; here, all feigned sluggishness is reprehensible, and all indulgent

---

33. On the debate on Robespierre see Haydon and Doyle, *Robespierre*.

34. Chaliand and Blin, *The History of Terrorism from Antiquity to al Qaeda*, 110.

35. Edelstein, "The Law of 22 Prairial: Introduction," 82–91.

or superfluous formality is a public threat. The delay for punishing enemies of the homeland should only be the time it takes to identify them; it is less a matter of punishing than annihilating them. A revolution like ours is nothing more than a quick succession of conspiracies, because this revolution is the war of tyranny against liberty, of crime against virtue. Instead of wasting time with examples, it is either a matter of exterminating the implacable satellites of tyranny or of perishing with the republic. Indulgence toward them is an atrocity, clemency is parricide.[36]

It is, as the introduction states, "less a matter of punishing than annihilating them" making revolutionary justice into a creative instrument rather than a defender of the status quo. The law did accelerate the terror, creating a "Great Terror" within the "Reign of Terror" and probably also accelerating the downfall of Robespierre uniting all his opponents through the fear of a violent death. Terror accelerated not only the revolution but also its enemies.

The French Revolution 2: Anti-Robespierre

No more than 5 months after his speech on terror and virtue, and seven weeks after the law, on 28 July 1794, Robespierre ended his days in the same guillotine which has become almost synonymous with his name. When he stood in the National Assembly the day before his execution defending himself, he used the concept of terror negatively, as a description of a fear and horror he didn't believe to have caused, terror in the sense of general shock and horror:

> What, *we*, objects of terror to patriots? . . . *we*, objects of terror to the National Convention . . . It is at *us* the assassin's dagger is aimed, yet *we* it is who are painted as objects of terror. . . . To appear an object of terror in the eyes of those we revere and love is, for a man of feeling and probity, the most frightful of tortures.[37]

It is as if he senses the shift in meaning about to take place. More important, his opponents wanted to connect him with despotism and thereby with arbitrary and excessive violence but they couldn't just call it terror as they had previously consented, or at least not seriously objected, to Robespierre's linkage of terror and virtue into a legitimate instrument of state violence

36. "The Law of 22 Prairial," 93–94.
37. Bienvenu, *The Ninth of Thermidor*, 145 and 147.

which also continued after his death in the much less known and repudiated "white terror." It is very saying of the non-necessary connection between act and description that the downfall of Robespierre, the end of "the terror," meant that he and twenty others were guillotined together with 71 the next day making it the highest number in one day during the entire period. Denis Richet remarks: "The Terror could not be ended without more terror."[38] In fact, the counter-terror showed itself every bit as brutal and ferocious as the terror it combated and succeeded.[39] Instead of accusing him of terror they invented a new word, "terrorism," which came to mean illegitimate use of politically motivated violence, this time about a (albeit illegitimate) state power but later more frequently used about non-state actors who by definition in the state era is illegitimate users of violence.

It is only with this shift that the modern usage of the concept of terror becomes fully visible as terror. It is hereafter increasingly reserved for the kind of fear coming from political violence rather than from any of the other possible sources of fear and horror and even more pointedly, from illegitimate violence wielded by despots (dictatorships or totalitarian states) or by individuals (terrorists). It is only through this conceptual change that terror as violence can come to mean a systematic and premeditated violence against society. Terror comes to mean violence not *from the state against individuals* but violence *from despots or terrorists against state and society*. One mustn't of course expect a complete reversal of meaning and there is a significant amount of different temporalities in conceptual usage but the transformation of terror in its political sense from a state practice to an illegitimate non-state or illegitimate state practice is quite clear. Even though Thuriot a few days after Robespierre's execution speaks about terror as "the blade of law"[40] the general transformation from neutrality before Robespierre, to legitimacy during Robespierre, and to illegitimacy after is easily documented.

The word "terrorism" was itself first used in the French National Assembly in August 1794 by Jean-Lambert Tallien who himself had overseen the reign of terror in the provinces but met a suspected attack for being corrupt and excessively violent from Robespierre by attacking first (he had used the term "system of terror" the day after Robespierre's execution).[41]

---

38. Richet, "Coups d'état," 14.
39. Andress, *The Terror*, chapter 12.
40. Bienvenu, *The Ninth of Thermidor*, 218.
41. Baczko, *Ending the Terror*, 342, 366, 384.

He was the first to describe the reign of terror as a "system of power" put in place by Robespierre (in 1791, however, Thomas Paine in his *Rights of Man* had described a "government by terror.").[42] What we see is a man culpable of corruption and terror engineering the later prevailing conception of the reign of terror and its intimate relation to Robespierre's name. What Tallien does is to name 'the terror' the same as its supposed adversary, despotism. He says:

> This system of Terror supposes the exercise of an arbitrary power in those who undertake to spread terror. It also supposes absolute power, and I mean by absolute power one that owes obedience or justification to no one, and which demands it of everyone else . . . The system of Terror supposes the most concentrated power, the power that approaches closest to uniformity and tends inevitably to royalty.[43]

The word "terrorist" is also used for the first time in this period. A Jacobin sans-culotte, Hébert, reprimanded for being a terrorist responded in May 1794:

> Doubtless I am a Terrorist, but I gave proof of this only before the castle of the tyrant Capet on 10 August 1792, where my terrorism cost me my left arm . . . I am a man of blood. But I was lavish only with my own blood on August 10, the loss of which I have regretted only because it kept me from fighting at the frontiers with my brothers.[44]

Terrorism and terrorist is here neutral or even honorable terms. But the dominant interpretation of "terrorist" was that of *Le Courrier francais*, July 1795:

> It is not without reason that all the sections of Paris demands of the convent that the terrorists be convicted. The ease by which the doors of the prison are opened for them must make good citizens fear that these bloodthirsty devils once again will come to cause political turbulence among us.[45]

Any suggestion reminiscent of the Jacobins was declared to be terroristic, as when someone in May 1795 proposed to vote by roll call. He was thrown

42. Paine, *The Rights of Man*, 24.
43. Baczko, *Ending the Terror*, 51.
44. Soboul, *The Sans-Culottes*, 24.
45. Furet and Richet, *La Révolution francaise*, 310.

out of the Assembly by an almost unanimous vote calling him a "notorious Terrorist."[46] This hysteria seem to indicate a deeply felt although probably unconscious desire to rid oneself of complicity in the terror by naming "terrorists" just as on "14 Thermidor [1 August 1794], again to 'loud applause', the Convention abolished the law of 22 Prairial, symbol and legal base of the 'great Terror'. By their loud applause the deputies seemed to want to exorcize the memory of their own vote" for the Prairal law.[47] With this we witness the transformation of terror from a state maxim into a term of abuse and furthermore from a state of mind, terror as fear and horror in the individual, into something one can be: a terrorist.

The general consensus is formulated by Barère on 1 August 1794: "Terror was always the arm of despotism; justice is the arm of liberty."[48] Still, a few days before, on 29 July 1794 he used "terrify" in a positive sense:

> Let the people always find here equality in laws, and liberty in means, let the revolutionary movement not hesitate on its purifying course; and let the Convention still terrify traitors and kings, conspirators within and despotic governments without. Then our effort will continue, the secret triumphs of our armies' political enemies, steeped in conspiracy, will be brought to naught: and victory's triumphal chariot will roll over the corpses of our enemies and over soil which still knows slaves and masters.[49]

The quote expresses a revolutionary and state of exception logic not unlike Robespierre's which may explain the use of the very Robespierrean sentence to "terrify traitors and kings, conspirators within and despotic governments without" (Barère had also sat on the 12 man Committee of Public Safety with Robespierre and Saint-Just which from September 1793 to July 1794 operated under the motto "revolutionary until peace"[50]). This, however, mustn't obscure the general direction of things, the now prevailing consensus in the National Assembly was, as Tallien says on August 1794 that "terror is the weapon of tyranny."[51]

46. Soboul, *The Sans-Culottes*, 142.
47. Baczko, *Ending the Terror*, 62.
48. Walther, "Terror, Terrorismus," 347; Bienvenu, *The Ninth of Thermidor*, 264.
49. Bienvenu, *The Ninth of Thermidor*, 247–48.
50. Gershoy, *Bertrand Barere*; Palmer, *The Age of the Democratic Revolution*,112.
51. Bienvenu, *The Ninth of Thermidor*, 92.

In the following exchange of remarks from the National Assembly on 19 August 1794 we find what we may take as the decisive moment in the conceptual transformation making terror into illegitimate violence:

> *Louchet:* Deeply impressed with the immensity of the perils which still threaten the public liberty and with the necessity to eliminate as soon as possible the source of our domestic disturbances; persuaded that for this there exists no other means than to maintain terror everywhere as the order of the day—(violent murmurs interrupt the speaker; from all parts of the hall burst out the words Justice! Justice!) By the word 'terror', I mean the severest justice.

> *Charlier:* Justice for the patriots, terror for the aristocrats.

> *Many voices:* Justice for everyone (applause) It is justice that will terrify the aristocrats and guarantee the patriots.

> *Louchet:* It never entered my heart to make terror the order of the day. I move that the severest justice repress the infamous aristocracy and the slack moderatism, which everywhere are raising their insolent heads (a few murmurs) . . .

> *Tallien:* . . . I shall content myself with remarking that the Convention did not approve all the principles contained in this speech, that it did not approve the statement that terror must be made the order of the day. I shall express myself with the frankness I have already shown; I repeat what I have already said: Terror is the weapon of tyranny. (applause) The severest justice must be used against all our country's enemies. (applause) Robespierre also used to say constantly that terror must be made the order of the day, and while with the aid of these words he had patriots incarcerated and led to the scaffold, he protected the rascals who were serving him. Yes, the Convention must strike them down; it is against these robbers of the public that it must wage eternal war. I no longer recognize castes in the republic; I see in it only good and bad citizens. (applause).[52]

The end of the Jacobin regime is then also the (beginning of the) end of the positive use of the concept of terror but it keeps its new element of creative violence in the service of a new society. What is even more important is the *opposition between terror and justice*, between regimes surviving on the use of terror and regimes constituted by the rule of law. This opposition becomes very operational later, not least in the cold war. As Walter

---

52. Bienvenu, *The Ninth of Thermidor*, 304–5.

Lacqueur summarizes the situation after Robespierre's execution: "[T]errorist became a term of abuse with criminal implications."[53]

An important part of the conceptual transformation was the use of terror as an epochal concept in the "Reign of Terror," now understood as a state-sanctioned use of violence against one's own population. Turning it into a epochal concept served as a way to distance oneself from the newly established stigma of terror by relegating it to the past of someone else thereby avoiding having to contemplate the terroristic dimensions of one's own system of repression. Terror was now effectively becoming the work always of someone else.

Terror was now understood as what former justice minister Dominique Garat called a "système exterminateur" [system of extermination] or as the new edition of *Dictionnaire de l' Académie française* in 1798 called "système, régime de la terreur" [system, regime of terror]; likewise "terrorist" came to mean someone who wanted to reinstate the Jacobin regime and later a common conservative critique of the French revolution and the claim that all attempts to "bring heaven down on earth" will result in terror. This is also how Immanuel Kant uses it in *Streit der Fakultäten* from 1798 where he speaks of the "terrorist idea of human history" [der terroristische Vorstellungsart der Menschengeschichte][54] meaning an idea about the future which predicts the increasingly worse, the continuous decline, just as the anti-Robespierreans depicted the descent of the terror into the duplication of what it was meant to replace.

Terror in counter-enlightenment discourse

Not in the Enlightenment but still an integral part of the European debate was Edmund Burke, who drew a connection between terror and the sublime in *Ideas of the Sublime and the Beautiful* from 1757, but which I'll leave unexamined.[55] In his political writings we find the concept used about the deterrent effect of laws, for example in *Thoughts on the Cause of the Present Discontents* from 1770, in which he laments the fact that "the laws are despoiled of all their respected and salutary terrors."[56] It is in the

53. Lacqueur, *The Age of Terrorism*, 11.

54. Kant, "Streit der Fakultäteten," 353.

55. Battersby, "Terror, terrorism and the sublime"; Neocleous, "The Monstrous Multitude."

56. Burke, "Thoughts on the Cause of the Present Discontents," 125.

same text also, among others, used for England's ability to strike "terror in rival nations"[57] and for a political school filled with "effectual terror of the growth of an aristocratic power."[58] In a speech on America from 1774, criticizing the British parliament's handling of the American case, he talks of a session of parliament, 1768, full of "idle terror and empty menaces" and he castigates the parliament for firstly having used violence and then stopped it prematurely: "You began with violence; and before terrors could have any effect, either good or bad, your ministers immediately begged pardon."[59]

Most important and influential were Burke's use of the concept in connection with the French Revolution. In his masterpiece, *Reflections on the Revolution in France* from 1790, the concept of terror is used very broadly and without any apparent directly political content, that is in this case without restricting its use to the fear others purposively instil. It is used about statesmen-like politicians of former times: "They were men of great civil, and great military talents, and if the terror, the ornament of their age."[60] And it is also used about the French National Assembly:

> It is notorious, that all their measures are decided before they are debated. It is beyond doubt, that under the terror of the bayonet, and the lamp-post, and the torch to their houses, they are obliged to adopt all the crude and desperate measures suggested by clubs composed of a monstrous medley of all conditions, tongues, and nations.[61]

In this new state of affairs Burke has no confidence in man's natural abilities and passions, which he imagines the new government at war with. Having destroyed man's natural commitments and virtues only naked self-interest moves man:

> On the scheme of this barbarous philosophy, which is the offspring of cold hearts and muddy understandings, and which is as void of solid wisdom, as it is destitute of all taste and elegance, laws are to be supported only by their own terrors, and by the concern, which each individual may find in them, from his own private speculations, or can spare to them from his own private interests.[62]

57. Ibid., 135.
58. Ibid., 136.
59. Burke, "Speech on American Taxation," 103.
60. Burke, *Reflections on the Revolution in France*, 136.
61. Ibid., 160.
62. Ibid., 171.

He also talks at great length about "the terrors of this tremendous proscription" which is the confiscation of church property,[63] describing terror not as an instrument but as a cause. This is perhaps implied later when he says that the French "hope to secure their constitution by a terror of a return of those evils which attended their making it,"[64] which I read as a reference to revolutionary violence. Even though the quotes may indicate it, Burke does not reserve the concept of terror to its political usage or to what others do. His use indicates only that he views the new French government as terrible and horrible. He is not linking it directly with the concept of terror. He even refers to its religious usage saying that our minds "are purified by terror and pity"[65] and he talks of a king's ascension to the throne as implying a recovery of "his first terrors,"[66] that is the fear of taking on the royal obligations.

A year later it seems a monopolization of the concept to illegitimate violence is occurring when he in *A Letter to a Member of the National Assembly* from 1791 coldly remarks: "Your despots govern by terror" and he then adds an interesting remark:

> They know that he who fears God fears nothing else; and therefore they eradicate from the mind . . . that only sort of fear which generates true courage. Their object is, that their fellow-citizens may be under the domination of no awe but that of their Committee of Research and of their *lanterne*.[67]

With the danger of anachronism one can here observe a difference being described between true and benign religious fear and illegitimate and malignant political terror; and we can draw a parallel to descriptions of totalitarian states for not accepting rival sources of fear, least of all religion.

In an article of the same year, he writes that the new French rulers have introduced a new element into the diplomatic relations among nations, a condemnation of all other nations. They have sent a message of "terror and superiority" before shipping out ambassadors and he remarks that "the terror of France has fallen upon all nations."[68] He is still not restricting the use of the concept of terror to his revolutionary opponents but

63. Ibid., 223.
64. Ibid., 301.
65. Ibid., 175.
66. Ibid., 320.
67. Burke, "A Letter to a Member of the National Assembly," 622.
68. Burke, "Thoughts on French Affairs," 249 and 252.

this seems to happen in the following years, although the transformation is, of course, not complete.

In 1793 he talks of "the terrours of the present power are such as no regular Government can possibly employ" and he says that the new government has made "the effects of mere terrour" into "a principle"[69] making the connection between despotism and terror that we saw earlier. One should also remark that Burke in his writings just after 1789 more often uses the concept of despotism than terror to describe the new government and its policies.

Three years on, in 1796, in *The First Letter on a Regicide Peace* the French government has become a "scourge and terror" and he speaks of "the palpable night of their terrors"[70] but still uses the concept more broadly as a synonym of fear as evident in the subsequent three letters on a regicide peace, where he talks about the West Indian barbarian's "cannibal terror"[71] about the British navy being formerly "the terror of the world"[72] and in the fourth letter from 1797 he uses on the same page terror to describe both what the regicide power does, what it is ("the moral terrors of this successful empire of barbarism") and to describe a kind of panic in the British which paralyzes action.[73] This fourth letter is also where we find Burke using the word 'terrorist' for the first time:

> To secure them [the French revolutionaries] further, they have a strong corps of irregulars, ready armed. Thousands of those hell-hounds called Terrorists, whom they had shut up in prison, on their last revolution, as the satellites of tyranny, are let loose on the people. The whole of their government, in its origination, in its continuance, in all its actions, and in all its resources, is force; and nothing but force.[74]

In this quote we see Burke using the anti-Robespierrean 'terrorist' without acknowledging any change in the violent and regicide system of France. Just as much as everyone else, if not more, the counter-enlightenment helped fashion the modern concept of terror, not least did they help make the connection between revolution and terror which has followed every

69. Burke, "Remarks on the Policy of the Allies," 282 and 286.
70. Burke, "First Letter on a Regicide Peace," 289 and 291.
71. Burke, "Second Letter on the Regicide Peace," 189.
72. Burke, "Third Letter on the Regicide Peace," 228.
73. Burke, "Fourth Letter on the Regicide Peace," 337.
74. Ibid., 370.

revolutionary movement since as an a priori accusation of the terrorist consequences of unbounded political ambitions.[75] Not only the counter-enlightenment but also the widespread European and American horror at the "terroristic excesses" of the revolution[76] served to consolidate terror as an abominable kind of violence perpetrated by despotisms (later totalitarians) and their revolutionary counterparts actually mimicking the regime they were supposedly fighting, turning into despotisms or dictatorships themselves. The revolution eating itself is revolution becoming despotic just as it is revolutionary violence becoming despotic terror.[77]

Terror, terrorism, terrorist

In an article on the revolutionary terror Claude Lefort, examining closely a speech by Robespierre, says:

> Whatever the statistical truth may be [about the number of dead during the French Revolution], no one can claim that the use of terror as a system of government or as a temporary means of enslavement was an invention of the French Revolution; in previous centuries, the same system had been used against groups who were deemed to be heretical, or who simply refused to pay taxes.[78]

This is very true but as I have tried to show this is not really what terror comes to mean: just an instrument of police or exception. It has obvious parallels in history but the French Revolution inaugurated something new which Lefort hints at just after the quotation above: "The Revolutionary Terror *speaks*. It implies self-justification, a debate as to its function, its ends and even its limits." The truly new in the revolutionary terror which separates it from all other previous instances of terror is exactly that it speaks, that it wants to convince, or more precisely put: it wants to convince not by reference to what is, as all previous terror, but to what must come. It speaks because it wants to change something. It's a terror not solely or even primarily concerned with subduing its victims but in convincing its spectators (and most possibly also its perpetrators).

75. McMahon, *Enemies of the Enlightenment*, chapter 3; Thorup, *Fornuftens perversion*.

76. Musolff, "Schreckenswörter an der Tagesordnung"; Luzzatto, "European Visions of the French Revolution."

77. Calvert, "Terror in the Theory of Revolution," chapter 2.

78. Lefort, "The Revolutionary Terror," 70.

Whereas the concept of terror was formerly used about the barbaric or deterrent use of state violence, the psychological dispositions of individuals, religious and social fear etc. in the period after the French Revolution the conceptual usage is prioritized as a description of non-state violence aimed at the state or the citizens which the state is obligated to protect. Terror is externalized from the state (the concept of "state terror" doesn't name the state but only the excessive state as terroristic just like "police violence" doesn't name the police violent but only that which exceeds the mandated violence). In a sense the concept of terror keeps being a state concept, but now it becomes the state description of private use of (now) illegal violence; a transformation we can summarize as the move *from terror as state practice to terror as terrorism*. Terror is no longer solely a concept of the emotion caused by scaring incidents but is rather becoming the act which in itself causes fear.

2

Speaking the Bomb: Karl Heinzen and the Invention of the Terrorist Language

VIOLENCE HAS A VOICE. Through history, various discourses have reconciled the violent actor with his (and sometimes her) violence. The history of violence is the history of religious, political, philosophical and literary descriptions of "good" and "bad" violence. Where one finds violence, voice is never far away. This is no debate among equals, however. The state is a privileged voice. Non-state violent actors struggle to formulate a language enabling the powerless to confront the powerful.

In 1853 a small pamphlet, *Murder and Liberty*, was published by a largely unknown author, Karl Heinzen (1809–1880).[1] The pamphlet generated little attention and its author is mostly known because Marx and Engels at some point criticized him for bourgeois tendencies. Neither pamphlet nor author played any significant role in the history of violence. However, one can read the pamphlet symptomatically as an expression of the need for bringing the language of violence from the age of the tyrant to the age of the state. Heinzen's pamphlet is an interesting transitional document from then still-active tyrannicidal traditions to the language of modern terrorism. The pamphlet is interesting for not being part of the modern radical traditions, most notably anarchism, most often associated with early modern terrorism.

---

1. Heinzen, *Murder and Liberty*.

What this small case study demonstrates is that contrary to present usage and common understanding, terrorist language came into being in defense of personal liberty and democracy—not as an attack on those values. The title of Heinzen's pamphlet indicates as much: the title is murder *and* liberty, not murder *or* liberty. The article aims to explore Heinzen's pamphlet as one indicator of the emergence of the terrorist language as a pro-democracy discourse, situating his discourse within the changing parameters of legitimate violence moving from personalist to systemic rule and exploring the basic contours of modern languages of political violence in general. The article trails the development from a "language of the dagger" to a "language of the bomb," i.e., from the personal tyrannicide to the beginnings of terrorism seeing "systemtic" enemies. My purpose is not to explain the emergence of terrorism as a political tactic but to document the development of a legitimating language "suitable" for such a murderous practice. Heinzen is, I will argue, a perfect representative of the shift in language from tyrannicide to terrorism.

On Karl Heinzen

Heinzen was born 1809 in Grevenbroich in Düsseldorf as son of a forester.[2] He studied medicine as well as literature. However, he thrown out of the University of Bonn in 1829 for criticizing the lack of academic freedom (the reality is that he may have been removed due to lack of academic performance). Heinzen's subsequent military service, partly as a mercenary in Dutch East India, fortified his anti-authoritarianism. He then fell in love. Needing a steady income, he became a bureaucrat in the Prussian administration (1833-1844). His fiancé died in 1835, leaving behind four children whom Heinzen supported. He married the eldest daughter in 1839. In this period as civil servant his political inclination was towards liberal democracy, advocating for freedom of the press as well as administrative and constitutional reforms. Via his propagandizing, Heinzen found trouble, and his political beliefs radicalized.

During his civil service years, Heinzen came into contact with the Young Hegelians. He admired Marx in particular, though they are never friends.[3] Marx and Heinzen a very personal feud, in fact, after Heinzen

2. The following is based on Huber, *Karl Heinzen* and Wittke, "Karl Heinzen's Literary Ambitions."

3. Wittke, *Against the Current*, 236–40.

in 1847 published an article in *Deutsche-Brüsseler-Zeitung* criticizing communism. First Engels[4] and then Marx[5] responded harshly, describing Heinzen as a petit-bourgeois functionary with no understanding of economics or politics. In 1849 Engels denounced Heinzen in a letter to the editor of the *Northern Star* and denied that he should in any way be considered a "shining light of the German Social Democratic party."[6] Heinzen's name was often used by English conservatives to attack the German community in Britain, its radical circles not the least, because of a pamphlet, *Lehren der Revolution*, advocating mass murder in the service of the revolution.

A significant part of conservative critique, contempt even, concerned Heinzen's idea that the crowned heads of Europe bore primary guilt for poverty and misery. Marxists were also harsh on Heinzen; Marx and Engels accuse Heinzen of maintaining a purely moralistic critique of state power in a limited sense, wherein he in fact serving capitalism by misdirecting the justified anger of the working class. Heinzen was, according to Marx and Engels, too caught up in personalist interpretations of oppression, obscuring its systemic nature. Finally, Marx and Engels accuse Heinzen of a fetishizing combat by oft-substituting analysis with constant calls to action.

In the 1840s, Heinzen began writing books and pamphlets, one of them landing him at court for criticizing the Prussian bureaucracy. Before the trial date in 1844, Heinzen fled to Belgium, marking the definitive start of his radicalization. At this point, Heinzen argued for a belief that only revolution could bring about a liberal-democratic republic.

In exile, Heinzen became an outspoken advocate for revolution in Germany, smuggling pamphlets into the country. In 1848 he set out for America, greeted among sections of the emigrant German-American community as revolutionary authority. In Philadelphia there was even a parade welcoming him. The influx of German revolutionaries to America was at this time not thought of as a failure for revolution in Germany but as a sign that it was imminent.[7] After only two weeks in the U.S., the 1848-revolution broke out in France. Europe seemed on the verge of a major upheaval. Heinzen hurried back to the continent only to become disenchanted over the failed revolutions. Once again he concludes that only actual, that is violent, revolution can bring about real change. Nothing is stronger than

4. Engels, "The Communists and Karl Heinzen."
5. Marx, "Moralising Criticism and Critical Morality."
6. Engels, "Letter to the editor of the Northern Star."
7. Wittke, *Refugees of Revolution*, 29–30.

thwarted expectations and destroyed hopes. These leave Heinzen with profound fatalism, nihilism, and an embittered resolve.

In 1849, Heinzen wrote the first of a number of texts later becoming "Murder and Liberty"—among them the article "Mord" ("Murder") in the February issue of *Die Evolution* (originally called *The Revolution* but, due to censure, the "R" was removed from the title). Here, he wrote: "We do not desire *any* killing, *any* murder, but if our enemies are not of the same mind, if they can justify murder, even go so far as to claim a special privilege in the matter, then necessity compels us to challenge this privilege."[8] Challenging the privileged and their claim to exercise the only just violence become an important theme for Heinzen—still more for "terroristic generations" after him. Not wanting to use violence oneself but confronting someone inherently violent became the standard argument for disassembling state claims that there is an intimate and necessary connection between legality and legitimacy rationally grounded only in the state.

Heinzen returned to America in 1850. Here, freedom of the press allowed him to express himself in the numerous short-lived journals and papers he came to edit.[9] Heinzen became one of the radical voices of the so-called German Forty-Eighters, that is, Germans who immigrated to America around 1848 because of either political persecution or worsened living conditions.[10] Many Forty-Eighters adhered to enlightenment traditions of rationalism and materialism. Forty-Eighters tended to be anti-clerical and anti-authoritarian. In the Forty-Eight milieu, Heinzen was one of the activists advocating abolition of slavery, equal rights for women, science over religion, self-determination over authority.[11] His radical stance on many issues, especially his fierce and consistent defense of equal rights for women and blacks made him many enemies. This was even among radicals, who had inconsistent opinions on gender and race. Heinzen fought not least with the communists among the emigrant milieu. Heinzen turned Marxian critique on its head and accused communists of for economism and singularly focusing on capitalism as the cause of misery: "Not hatred against

8. Heinzen, "Murder."

9. Wittke, *Against the Current*, 275-276.

10. Wittke, "The German Forty-Eighters in America"; Brancaforte, *The German Forty-Eighters*; Levine, *The Spirit of 1848*.

11. For a description of Heinzen's close friend, the prominent female physician Marie Elizabeth Zakrzewska and the political and scientific ideas of the German Forty-Eighters see Tuchman, "Only in a Republic."

capital, but hatred against *oppression* [should be] the saving watchword."[12] Heinzen called himself a socialist, yet one accepting basic tenets of capitalism and private property. He asserted: "I do not wish to destroy individual property rights. I only wish to see that they are safeguarded for all."[13]

Settled in America, Heinzen turned his attention to reforming American politics rather than German. His ideas about implementing radical reform in America are evident from a speech held on Independence Day 1876. Here, he sharply criticizes repression towards blacks and women, arguing in favour of a democratic reform, a republican, truly undivided government and replacing the presidency and the senate with "an assembly of agents or deputies of the people, in permanent session, who may be instructed by their constituents, or replaced by others, at any time."[14] Heinzen wanted a bill of rights, important issues put to a popular vote and independent courts "subject to the control of the people."[15] Heinzen was throughout his life a consistent critic of repression towards blacks and women, accusing Lincoln and his emancipation acts of not being radical enough, as well as emphasizing the difference between an "andro-cracy" (excluding women) and "true democracies" of a "*whole* population dwelling upon the soil of the State."[16] Heinzen also agitated for atheism and materialism as the only true humanism liberating man from metaphysical forces of a religious nature.[17] Summarizing Heinzen's beliefs, he was a liberal democrat coming to the conclusion, at least in relation to Europe, that violence was the only way to democracy and the rule of law. Regarding America, Heinzen seems to have opted for a reformist approach. He was engaged in attempts at party building,[18] including a first attempt at a national organization of the Forty-Eighters (the Louisville Platform of 1854). This divided German-Americans into a radical section, supporting the platform, and a moderate one opposing it.[19] The Platform advocated equality of race, class and gender,

---

12. Heinzen, *Communism and Socialism*.

13. In Levine, *The Spirit of 1848*, 45.

14. Heinzen, *What is Real Democracy?*, 62-63.

15. Heinzen, *Lessons of a Century*. See also his *The True Character of Humboldt*.

16. Heinzen, *What is Real Democracy?*, 10.

17 Heinzen, *What is Humanity?* For a full list of Heizen's publications, see Friesen, '*Trotz alledem und alledem.*'

18. Nagler, "The Lincoln-Fremont Debate"; Levine, *The Spirit of 1848*, 150, 216, 247.

19. Kleber, *The Encyclopedia of Louisville*, 564–65; Honeck, *We are the Revolutionists*, 29.

expressed a deep dissatisfaction with what was seen as the broken promises of the American Declaration of Independence. The Platform called for free land to all actual settlers and an end to the clerical influence on public life, abolition of federalism, the presidency and senate as well as administrative, social and penal reform.[20]

Throughout his lifetime, Heinzen wrote poetry; this is also how he is most remembered, despite his active politics and radical view of violence.[21] Heinzen died in Boston in 1880, as unknown as he is today. Since Carl Wittke's biography, Against the Current from 1945, Hienzen is practically only mentioned in connection with the German Forty-Eighters, there being only a few academic articles on his revolutionary writings.[22] Attention paid to the anarchists as forerunners of contemporary terrorism or of terrorism as such seems to have pushed Heinzen and others like him into obscurity. This paved the way for sanitized liberal-democratic narratives of peaceful path to democracy. Heinzen did have some influence on the German-American anarchists. Twentty years after his death, in the September issue of the German-American anarchist journal Freiheit, one of the fathers of anarchist terrorism, Johann Most, published excerpts from Heinzen's pamphlet "Murder and Liberty." The issue came out only hours before an alleged anarchist Leon Gzolgosz shot and killed the American president William McKinley on September 6, 1901. Publicizing Heinzen's plea for the murder of tyrants at this inopportune moment led to Most's arrest as a spiritual force behind the assassination. This lead to a one year prison sentence.[23]

Tyrannicide and terrorism

Heinzen's pamphlet is filled with references to tyrannicides. Brutus, Tell and others are presented as contemporaries in the sense that their example

20. Jentz, "The 48ers and the Politics," 50–52; Wittke, Against the Current, 163-165.

21. Huber, Karl Heinzen; Wittke, Against the Current, 73; Wittke, "Karl Heinzen's Literary Ambitions"; Neue Deutsche Biographie.

22. Laqueur, The Political Psychology of Appeasement, 89–99; Grob-Fitzgibbon, "From the dagger to the bomb"; Bessner and Stauch, "Karl Heinzen and the Intellectual Origins of Modern Terror." The latter article includes a re-translation of "Murder and Liberty."

23. New York Court of Special Sessions, "The People of the State of New York"; Fine, "Anarchism and the Assassination of McKinley"; Nomad, Apostles of Revolution, 275–99; Most's letters in prison is published in Harvey, "Johann Most in Prison."

is thought to have direct relevance for Heinzen's age. But the pamphlet also transcends the tyrannicide tradition in ways pointing into a subsequent "age of terror." We will here examine Heinzen's use of tyrannicide as well as how and why he has to depart from what serves as the leading argumentative structure of his text. First, however, we need to understand the tyrannicide tradition.

Tyrannicide is one of the great European violent traditions. Melvin Richter is correct to say that "the concept of tyranny is unique in its evocation of justifications for using violent means to deal with this type of regime."[24] In ancient Greece and Rome, tyrannicide was often hailed as a civic duty. This is one of the reasons why Thomas Hobbes, in his defense of royal absolutism, criticizes his contemporaries for reading Greek and Roman authors. In the famous chapter in *Leviathan*, "Of the Liberty of Subjects," where Hobbes mobilizes a negative concept of liberty against a republican understanding stressing citizen participation,[25] Hobbes scolds the educational tradition of Europe for reading these ancient authors:

> And by reading of these Greek, and Latine Authors, men from their childhood have gotten a habit (under a false shew of Liberty) of favouring tumults, and of licentious controlling the actions of their Soveraigns; and again of controlling those controllers, with the effusion of so much blood; as I think I may truly say, there was never any thing so deerly bought, as these Western parts have bought the learning of the Greek and Latine tongues.[26]

In *Behemoth*,[27] Hobbes singles out this reading as one of the causes of the English Civil War. More important still is that Hobbes writing in the 1650s and Heinzen writing in the 1850s both view this tradition as a motivating force for either tumult (Hobbes) or freedom (Heinzen). Hobbes represents an important negative interpretation of tyrannicide, emphasizing tyrannicide's disruptive features. Nonetheless, tyrannicide has often maintained a more positive interpretation as what James Tully, discussing John Locke's view on the right to rebel, calls "the activity of self-governing rebellion."[28] Locke describes this in his *Second Treatise* as follow:

24. Richter, "A Family of Political Concepts," 225.
25. Discussed in Skinner, *Liberty before Liberalism*.
26. Hobbes, *Leviathan*, 267.
27. Hobbes, *Behemoth*, 2–4.
28. Tully, *An Approach to Political Philosophy*, 46.

> The End of Government is the good of Mankind, and which us *best for Mankind*, that the People should be always expos'd to the boundless will of Tyranny, or that the Rulers should be sometimes liable to be oppos'd, when they grow exorbitant in the use of their Power, and imploy it for the destruction, and not the preservation of the Properties of their People?[29]

The right to rebel serves as both a warning creating an incentive to benign rule as well as corrective action when needed. Tyrannicide is the slaying of a tyrant for the common good; its legitimization is contingent upon an idea of a natural and just order violated by the tyrant. Tyrannicide has a restorative function and is a conservative and defensive institution. Tyrannicide's purpose is to restore entrenched values; tyrannicide does not to create new social institutions. The values of the tyrant-slayer have to reflect the values of the community just as the values of the tyrant contradict or subvert them.[30]

In its Greek and Roman, form tyrannicide was a means to an end. As David C. Rapoport writes in his *Assassination and Terrorism*, "its moral significance depended entirely on the *nature* of the person killed"[31] and not on the actual killing itself. Tyrannicide did, however, have to be committed for the right reasons. There was often a self-effacing element in just tyrannicide because the slayer couldn't expect to survive. Tyrannicide was 'justified killing' ending ideally in 'altruistic suicide.' Heinzen draws heavily on its purely instrumental or utilitarian evaluation in his re-interpretation. However, he also strongly departs from the suicidal dimension. Heinzen wants the morality of murder to be evaluated according to its end (freedom) rather than its means (murder). He wants his tyrant-slayers to survive to fight another day.

Despite the internal differences within the tyrannicide tradition there does seem to be consensus in describing the tyrant through either his usurpation or other unjust access to power (*ex defectu tituli*) or because of his actions when in office (*ex parte exercitii*). This means that the tyrant is subjectively guilty due to identifiable acts—he has violated common justice, God's laws, rules of succession or the like—whereas the one being attacked by terrorism is guilty due to his or her position rather than actions. In the latter case, the 'tyrant' attacked is only a representative of a system—the

---

29. Locke, *Two Treaties of Government*, 417.

30. Jászi and Lewis, *Against the Tyrant*, 91. See also Ford, *Political Murder*.

31. Rapoport, *Assassination and Terrorism*, 7.

system being the real target. Because one cannot literally 'bomb the system', one bombs the representatives of the system. This means that even though actual persons are being targeted, and perhaps their killing is legitimated by specific actions committed, the real target of the attack is not the person but the abstraction of the system.[32] In tyrannicide, one kills a person who's corrupting the system or society; in terrorism one attacks the system or society which has already corrupted everybody, including the 'tyrant'.

Tyrannicidal doctrines are dependent upon an order where power is personalized and immediately identifiable. The modern development towards what Quentin Skinner calls "the purely artificial person of the state"[33] challenges this notion of a personalized rule and, therein, any real notion of the tyrant. The idea of any one person solely responsible for the corruption and oppression loses credibility as power progressively becomes more systemic and administrative. Modernity changes power from throne to office, from king to minister, from sovereign to executive. Tyrants become increasingly irrelevant as socio-political and institutional practices make tyrannicide a less and less meaningful way to contemplate and attempt political violence. The idea of the tyrant and tyrannicide remains an active point of reference, as evident in the assassination attempt on Hitler in 1944. However, it can no longer serve as primary means of political violence because the murder of the 'tyrant' no longer promises the purpose of tyrannicide, the restoration of a violated justice.

Historically, the execution of the French king by the revolutionaries in 1793 marks the beginning of an interval between tyrannicide and terrorism. However, there had already been a shift away from the concept of tyranny in favour of the concept of despotism, most famously and importantly used by Montesquieu. This also signals a shift from locating the problem in the corrupt ruler to locating it in the system of governance.[34] The beheading of the Louis XVI drew in that sense lines both back in history and into the future. Revolutionaries drew heavily on the tyrannicide tradition, but not in a classical sense.[35] The king was executed less because of crimes committed than because he was king The institution of kingship which made him guilty. Execution happened no to right a wrong but to make a right.

32. Discussed in Miller, "The Intellectual Origins of Modern Terrorism."

33. Skinner, "Hobbes and the Purely Artificial Person of the State."

34. On Montesquieu's ideas of the oriental despotism see the illuminating book by Grossrichard, *The Sultan's Court.*

35. Walzer, *Regicide and Revolution.*

It was violence done not by one or a few suddenly stepping forward in the crowd to deliver a deadly blow, but rather in public by the "sovereign or revolutionary dictatorship" of the *pouvoir constituent*. Tyrannicide can be said to be a moment of "commissarial or restorative dictatorship," defending the purity of the constituent power.[36] This "suspends the constitution in order to protect the existence of the selfsame constitution," whereas the terrorism of the sovereign dictatorship "sees in the entire existing order the thing it wants to overthrow . . . It isn't directed at the present constitution but rather at the coming."[37] Hannah Arendt concurs:

> It is true, medieval and post-medieval theory knew of legitimate rebellion, of rise against established authority, of open defiance and disobedience. But the aim of such rebellions was not a challenge of authority or the established order of things as such; it was always a matter of exchanging the person who happened to be in authority, be it the exchange of an usurper for the legitimate king or the exchange of a tyrant who had abused his power for a lawful ruler.[38]

Political violence after the French Revolution concerned predominantly either the creation or prevention of a new order. Revolution took the place of tyrannicide as the premier legitimating reference of oppositional violence. Tyrannicide always concerns the ruler and society here and now; revolution always carries with a globalizing ambition intolerant of injustice and institutionalized, absolutist violence everywhere.[39]

Heinzen—as well as parts of the anarchist tradition—can be interpreted as transitory phenomena expressing the shift from personal to systemic power and concomitant changes in possibilities for "legitimate" rebellion. The Russian Socialist Revolutionaries and anarchists still targeted the Tsar and other authority figures accused of specific crimes, such as torture of fellow combatants or massacres of innocents[40]—this while simultaneously abandoning hope that one attack would decisively alter the social and political conditions. Both Heinzen and anarchists failed to integrate both new constellations of power and the emergence of mass politics into their doctrines. This was left to Lenin and the Bolsheviks to realize. The idea

36. Sieyès,"What is the Third Estate"; Breuer, "Nationalstaat und pouvoir constituant"; Preuss, "Constitutional Power-making"; Cristi, "Carl Schmitt on Sovereignty."

37. Schmitt, *Die Diktatur*, 133–34.

38. Arendt, *On Revolution*, 49.

39. Koselleck, *Critique and Crisis*; *Begriffsgeschichten*, 240–51.

40. Thorup, "The Anarchist and the Partisan"; Jensen, "The International Campaign."

of attacking the centre and the moral critique of specific rulers was still too attractive an option even though most came to realize its futility as a productive strategy. Tyrannicide became assassination and each attack only furthered the systemization of power and its conversion from despotic to bureaucratic dominance.[41]

The transition from tyrannicide to terrorism follows the depersonalization and systemization of power which is the modern territorial state. As stated above, Heinzen's text is interesting as a transitional document between a tyrannicide tradition targeting the "subjectively guilty" and a terroristic tradition targeting the "objectively guilty." The text is tension-ridden as Heinzen tries to reconcile these two perspectives while also trying to reflect and act upon the changes in the gap between the firepower of the state and the citizenry.

On *Murder and Liberty*

Heinzen's *Murder and Liberty* pamphlet is dedicated to the "the Peace League of Geneva." One should not, as Benjamin Grob-Fitzgibbon does in his article on Heinzen, look for such a league in the real world. It is an ironic comment on European states diplomatically agreeing on peace while preparing for war.[42] It is an irony reminiscent of the title of Immanuel Kant's *Zum ewigen Frieden* from 1795. Here, he explains, eternal peace was "written on the sign of a Dutch inn-keeper and on the sign was painted a grave yard."[43] Peace is not of this world; every 'peace league' is a way for the ruling powers to legitimate their rule by reference to peace; this while secretly preparing for war.

41. Mann, "The autonomous power of the state."

42. Grob-Fitzgibbon, "From the dagger to the bomb."

43. Kant, "Zum ewigen Frieden," 195. Notice also the introduction to Rousseau's "State of War" where he is critical of international law scholars writes: "I open the books on right and on ethics, I listen to the scholars and jurisconsults and, moved by their ingratiating discourses I deplore the miseries of nature, I admire the peace and justice established by the civil order, I bless the wisdom of public institutions, and console myself for being a man by seeing than I am a citizen. Fully instructed about my duties and happiness, I close the book, leave the class-rom, and look around me; I see unfortunate peoples groaning under an iron yoke, mankind crushed by a handful of oppressors, starving masses overwhelmed by pain and hunger, whose blood and tears the rich drink in peace, and everywhere the strong armed against the weak with the frightful power of the laws . . . Ah barbarous philosopher! Read us your book on a battlefield," Rousseau, "State of War," 162.

Heinzen starts by noting the paradox that violence is universally abhorred but also universally present.[44] He insists that a truly non-violent position must be against violence in all its forms. Heinzen challenges moral differentiations in which the state claims to own a different type of violence. The distinction between legal and illegal violence is not translatable to a moral distinction. By saying that the only genuine criteria is violence/non-violence, Heinzen is able to critique legalistic views of violence. This is also why Heinzen engages in a fictional dialogue with a judge and a soldier—the representatives of legal violence—thereby accusing the courts and war in general for being nothing *but* violence.[45] No distinctions or legal niceties should obscure the fact that violence is predominantly a state prerogative and that this doesn't make violence a lesser problem in actual or moral terms. Heinzen's exposes the hypocrisy of violent actors who only ever feel outraged about others' violence. In that same move, he explains explain the necessity of counter-violence to an audience already integrated into the state narrative.

Heinzen devotes special attention to the violence of the reigning powers. His whole text is a redescription of his age's politics as inherently and extraordinarily violent: "The large, blood-stained picture which we call history shows us murder in a thousand forms, and the murderers under a thousand names."[46] Institutionalized, or state, power is violent to an extent making revolutionary violence seem insignificant. That is not how we have been made to see it, however. State violence is portrayed—and to a significant extent accepted—as uninterrupted normality. Revolutionary or insurrectionary violence is seen as the disruptive introduction of violence into the community. It is this naturalization of state violence Heinzen seeks to disrupt. This in order both to delegitimize the state narrative of its unproblematic violence and to legitimize a counter-violence—the two minimal requirements of any insurrectionary attempt.

To make these arguments Heinzen uses the language of the tyrannicide tradition but with a twist signalling the transformation of power from the personal to the systemic. The idea of usurpation of power is transformed from an accusation that this particular tyrant has unjustly seized power to usurpation being the foundation of state power as such. Kings and ministers are but successful thieves who have disguised the violent source of their

44. Heinzen, *Murder and Liberty*, 1.

45. Ibid., 3.

46. Ibid., 5.

power and might behind a veil of legality. The idea of the abuse and corrupting influence of a tyrant in power is transformed from an accusation of this particular crime or transgression to a universal condemnation of this kind of power as such. Their guilt is not a specific crime; their existence is the source of the generalized societal corruption. Their existence is what brutalizes society. Their violence is only just the exterior confirmation of this fact.

It is through these transformations we must understand Heinzen's allegation that the "greatest of all follies of the world is the belief that *it is possible to commit a crime* against despots and their accomplices."[47] This language is reminiscent from the execution of Louis XVI stating that the issue is not a specific crime but the office of king itself. The folly, according to Heinzen, consists in unknowingly accepting the categories of power—established law and power versus crime—and use them to evaluate actions, possibly even one's own actions, against the power. It is not possible to commit a crime against despots because they are illegitimate in and of themselves. They are the actual outlaws of the just society. Power is illegitimate because it is grounded in usurpation and only sustained through violence; it can thus not claim protection or demand obedience. The power is a predator set free to devour the innocent. Heinzen frequently uses animal metaphors to describe the power as carnivorous and dangerous, drawing on a long tradition of suspicion of power often seen in early liberal thought, for instance in chapter seven of John Locke's *Second Treatise*, "Of Political or Civil Society." Here, he sharply criticizes those who think that "*absolute Power purifies Mens Bloods*" which is the same as believing that "to avoid what Mischiefs may be done them by *Pole-Cats*, or *Foxes*" they think "it Safety, to be devoured by *Lions*."[48]

Whereas Locke used this terminology to advocate a rule-based polity, for Heinzen such words enable him to portray rebellion as a self-defense necessitated by a generalized, systematized attack by power on the population. Self-defense is obviously a potent way to legitimate one's violence. Not only is the source of violence placed outside oneself; it also structures the field of action so that the only moral response is a counter-violence; emphatically a violence to halt violence. Using the images of an animalistic power and a defending populace were ways for Heinzen to subvert the

47. Ibid., 19.

48. Locke, *Two Treaties of Government*, 327–28. On predatory animals as political metaphors see Münkler, *Politische Bilder*, 93–124); on animals in political theory see Derrida, *The Beast and the Sovereign I*.

naturalization of statist perspectives. This is also why he drew so heavily on the tyrannicide tradition. Tyrannicide was a doctrine of just violence taught in schools and revered in public ceremony. Tyrannicide is a violent doctrine even celebrated by power itself. What Heinzen does, however, is transform tyrannicide *qua* restorative doctrine into one of rebellion. Heinzen has understood that the age of classical tyrannicide is over. A single kill will solve nothing. The augmentation of state power, the increase of state power's violent potential, makes the martyr act of tyrannicide meaningless. Power has "increased the number of martyrs so vastly, that martyrdom has ceased to have significance."[49] It is an empty gesture tantamount to suicide. The number of victims is so great that the tyrant-slayer is not even granted a posthumous recognition. He or she just disappears while power persists. As Heinzen writes:

> The supremacy of crime, the supremacy of violence, the supremacy of the sword, the rule of murder is so fully recognized, so well established, has become so 'legal' and universal, that its victims scarcely find a passing sympathy in quiet concealment. The maiden mourns the loss of her lover, the mother the loss of her son, who—accidently was also a martyr in the cause of freedom. This closes the drama; liberty takes no notice of it, and murder continues to rule undisturbed.[50]

In a sense, Heinzen wants a moral adaptation to new possibilities which don't limit themselves by an obsolete 'chivalrous' understanding of violence as the clash between two combatants fighting on equal terms. This is especially when one part, the state, has already adopted its morality and strategy to the new possibilities.

This has a number of consequences. One must, according to Heinzen, understand the moral arbitrariness of the means of violence, or perhaps violence's strategic morality. This means that the way the different weapons and tactics are morally structured corresponds to the needs of reigning powers. The state maintains a distinction between legitimate means of violence and illegitimate means which don't concern the violence of means but their utility for the state. Means deemed necessary, such as regimented armies and missiles, are described as legitimate and moral whereas those available to the rebels, such as bomb-throwing, assassination and poisoning, are described as immoral. The state enforces a moral distinction which

49. Heinzen, *Murder and Liberty*, 16.
50. Ibid., 16.

seriously undermines the morality and possibility of rebellion. Heinzen's response is to insist on the amorality of all violent means. None are benign or praiseworthy. Some are nonetheless effective and rebels should evaluate them instrumentally rather than morally—"the victory alone decides."[51] The morality of violent means lie in their purpose not their use. For Heinzen this is a questioning of state descriptive power and the liberation of rebellious struggle. It's powerful; what Heinzen does is free the rebellion from any other considerations than expedience. In that sense, he is finely tuned to notions such as "military necessity" suggesting that the prime consideration is the use of extreme force to end the conflict *sooner* as this will cost less lives and bloodshed than a prolonged struggle.[52] It's also a mode of thought, however, that leads to the vindication of terror.

Heinzen is driven by a sense of a revolution slipping away. This was his personal experience in 1848—and he generalizes it into a critique of the "ill-conceived humanity" of earlier revolutions and rebellions failing in "the complete annihilation of their enemies."[53] Earlier revolutions failed because they granted the kind of mercy to their opponents which they would never themselves receive from the state. This wrongheaded philosophy of murder, the restraint of murder in the revolutionary situation, is Heinzen's explanation of why an age of liberty has not arrived. Revolutionaries have stopped short of vigorously defending revolutions and they have accepted the categories of state practice by considering one's enemies not as someone to be defeated, but opponents whose recognition have been sought by fighting on their terms. He scolds revolutionary leaders for shying away from openly declaring themselves for murder and for wanting "to be 'genteel' revolutionists" who "fashion their ethics *in accordance with the judgment of those who oppose the revolution.*"[54] What Heinzen obviously senses is that even revolutionary leaders merely want to place themselves in power rather than do away with power as such.

It is a reflection on the process by which the populace is disarmed and the state militarized and where, in the same process, violent means are increasingly sophisticated, expensive and bloody. This process undermines

51. Ibid., 19.

52. This was used by the German General Staff in the First World War, which argued, "the only true humanity very often lies in a ruthless application" of violent means "because they attain the object of war as quickly as possible [and are] when closely considered the most human" (German General Staff, *War Book*, 6, 17).

53. Heinzen, *Murder and Liberty*, 10.

54. Ibid., 21.

the effectiveness of ordinary street battles with their simulation of counterposed armies making previous rebel battle tactics such as the barricade an invitation to slaughter. Heinzen's pamphlet ends with six fictitious examples of rebel action: the bombing of a train carrying the crowned heads of Germany, the use of explosive bullets for a guerrilla force, mines deployed in street battle, a conspiracy of revolutionary poisoners and an organization of assassins targeting heads of state and a bombing of Emperor Louis Napoleon.[55] These examples are meant as inspiration and reflection of possible successful strategies. However, what is most striking in the examples are the lack of awareness of what Heinzen demonstrates elsewhere: that the killing of single individuals will not ensure victory. In the end, Heinzen fails to sketch a new course for rebellious activity and resorts to the desperate hope of what we could call an accelerated or continuous tyrannicide answering the persistence of systems with continued campaigns of murder. Heinzen prepares his reader for a moral short-circuit by expelling morality from strategic and tactical considerations and portraying cruelty and murder as the only moral choice—"the road to humanity leads over the summit of cruelty. This is the inexorable law of *necessity* dictated to us by the reaction."[56] This effectively places all blame for all violence onto the enemy, unleashing a potentially guiltless mass violence.

For Heinzen, neither murder nor self-sacrifice seriously challenges an established system, or "legal," or "legitimate," system. This is why Heinzen approximates the shift from tyrannicide to terrorism by radically enlarging the number of targets for attack, the number of the guilty. It is no longer this or that person but also the circle around him that becomes vulnerable. The number of legitimate targets multiplies as not only the tyrant but also his surroundings and associates are corrupt. The despair of Heinzen's text is in no small measure due to the fact that he senses the "corruption" of the working class and, not least, labour leaders. These seeming "potential revolutionaries" have become system-integrated. The multiplication from tyrant to system is supplemented by an augmentation of those required to act. In the tyrannicidal age, murder of the tyrant was an individual and voluntary obligation. Heinzen makes rebellion a general obligation incumbent on everyone. Failure to accept this obligation is tantamount to either surrender or betrayal. The idea of the "traitor" points towards both the age of nationalism and an age of terrorism

55. Ibid., 25–30.
56. Ibid., 20–21.

Perfect alibies

In *Rebel*, Albert Camus starts by saying that there are two kinds of crime: the emotionally induced, "crimes of passion," and logically-contemplated, "crimes of logic." The difference is whether the crime is premeditated or not. Camus remarks that we live in an age of premeditation and perfect crime, an age that kills on purpose and never lacks a justification for violence: "Our criminals are no longer helpless children who could plead love as their excuse. On the contrary, they are adults and they have a perfect alibi: philosophy which can be used for any purpose—even for transforming murderers into judges."[57] Perfect alibis are what Heinzen set out to formulate and what all violent actors must publicize to turn their violence into politics.

The legitimization of violence is a matter of secular problems accessible to human intervention. Their alibis for violence are perfect: violence now has to serve non-violence. Camus' political project became to criticize these alibis. Here, we analyse them. Camus highlights the constant dilemma of any oppositional doctrine or movement. Any type of radical opposition makes itself guilty of committing violence. On the other hand, sheer passivity allows violence and oppression to continue. This seems to be the inescapable dilemma of any type of radical opposition. In a contemporary context, the "War on Terror," one of the main arguments for invading Iraq was to end to Saddam Hussein's threats against the region and the oppression of his own people. Conversely, the opposition against the war in Iraq had to face the reverse moral dilemma—i.e., that *not* going to war would allow the brutality of an existing dictatorship to continue unhindered.

At the end of the day, no significant violent enterprise anywhere is without a reference to world peace. No violence exists without reference to a future condition of less or no violence. In modernity, political violence has to answer, and thus answer to, the question of violence's continuation or discontinuation. The dilemma between legitimizing violence and serving non-violence was a problem Heinzen engaged in his pamphlet, challenging all subsequent violent actors.

Just as "the powers that be" have their violence legitimated, possibly even celebrated, rebels will too if they succeed. Rebels are only amoral in defeat. Rebels can push the violence to its maximum effect, confident in the vindication of their violence. Means of violence are but means—effective or not. If effective, means of violence will be remembered as a heroic

57. Camus, *The Rebel*, 3.

struggle for freedom—if ineffective, they are registered as crime and terrorism. Heinzen insists on the same moral measure for state and rebels—an insistence progressively harder to insist upon or even to think as the state enlarges its dominance. Violence, Heinzen insists, is violence. The only thing that can meaningfully differentiate violence is its consequence. Will violence lead to the continuation of violence (state power) or its end (revolution)? Every other consideration serves only the law of the sword.[58]

58. Heinzen, *Murder and Liberty*, 15.

II

State Histories of the Total Enemy

3

The Total State: The "Total" as Answer to Mass Society in Early 20ᵗʰ Century Thinking

IN 1888, FRIEDRICH NIETZSCHE wrote that liberalism had developed into a *Herden-vertierung*, i.e., people reduced to cattle. Liberalism no longer creates freedom, since, following Nietzsche, "it is war which elicits these effects [freedom], it is the war for liberal institutions which, as war, allows illiberal instincts to exist."[1] Now that the liberals are no longer fighting a social war against aristocrats, liberalism produces neither freedom nor greatness, but on the contrary, decay, the herd mentality, and mediocrity.

Therefore, Nietzsche's age was no longer defined by liberalism, but rather by the "labor question," and he wrote what a liberal of his time could just as well have written: "I simply cannot grasp what should be done with the European worker after having made him into a question. He is no longer striding forwards asking immodestly. He finally has great numbers on his side."[2]

Here, Nietzsche was dealing with a double theme that would come to characterize the next fifty years, namely the disappearance of the liberal age and the rise of the labor or majority question. In 1919, the English economist John Maynard Keynes published *The Economic Consequences of the Peace* with its powerful condemnation of Western statesmen, who after

---

1. Nietzsche, *Götzen-Dämmerung*, §38.
2. Ibid., §40.

the First World War prioritized the narrow interests of nations above those of peace and welfare. One of the book's claims was that life before the First World War was still hard but for the most part people were content. There had been openings for enterprising spirits from all of the social classes, adequate infrastructure and a withdrawal of the state in an open world. People could travel "to any country or climate without passport or other formality," and even more importantly, everyone "regarded this state of affairs as normal, certain, and permanent, except in the direction of further improvement, and any deviation from it as aberrant, scandalous, and avoidable."[3]

Like Nietzsche, Keynes noted the break with 19th century liberalism, a break with and a criticism of liberalism that had already begun in the decades before 1900, but which would become steadily stronger before and during the First World War, turning into one of the dominating ideas of the period between the World Wars. His observations of a transformation in the idea and status of liberalism led him to conclude that "the forces of the nineteenth century have run their course and are exhausted. The economic motives and ideals of that generation no longer satisfy us: we must find a new way and must suffer again the *malaise*, and finally the pangs of a new industrial birth."[4]

The politicians, academics, and intellectuals whom we will take a look at hereunder shared something of this analysis, namely that part which grasped the demise of liberalism as a relevant political ideology and organizational principle. They also shared an idea of a new industrial birth—pushed along by malaise and pangs—but they also perceived the crisis of liberalism as permanent and sought other concepts and ideas for a post-liberal age. The focus in this chapter is put on continental Europe, particularly Germany, France, and Italy in the period 1900-1935 and the goal is to analyze what we could call a post-liberal discourse, shared by many liberals but also by a multitude of non- and anti-liberal tendencies.

Reducing schematically, we can operate with a series of ideal typical liberalisms in the era, each of which had its own historical development: the *social liberals,* in particular in England and later in France, sought a compromise between classical liberalism and the social question; the *market liberals* including, e.g., Ludwig von Mises who refused any compromise and fought for a "pure" market liberalism; the *constitutional liberals* including

3. Keynes, *The Economic Consequences,* 9–10.
4. Ibid., 238.

e.g., Hans Kelsen for whom the liberal Weimar constitution—even if it ultimately failed—was an example of liberal constitutional thought that had real political consequences in the early 20th century; and finally a *liberal attitude* shared by a whole row of European intellectuals who were not necessarily party politically organized but stood for a basic liberal position and championed different versions of "individual freedom" as their common point.[5]

It is primarily on this last group and its critics that I will focus upon hereunder. The group is generally characterized by a disillusioned mistrust of liberalism, accepting one form or another of collectivism as inevitable—often viewing fascism, later Nazism, as being convenient or preferable alternatives to socialism or communism, two collective forces the social development seemed headed for. The focus of this chapter is not on liberalism as an ideology or practice, but rather the *conceptions of liberalism and its chances of survival.* The purpose is not to discuss or decide whether liberalism was in harmony with or in opposition to social developments in the first part of the 20th century, but rather to examine the trend-setting interpretation—shared amongst both liberals and anti-liberals—that the age of liberalism and individualism was over and that *the age of the total* was upon us.

The chapter starts with a very brief presentation of the status of liberalism in the decades around 1900 stressing in particular the growing consciousness of the crisis recognized by Nietzsche and later confirmed by Keynes. The second section takes a look at the sociological and psychological literature on the masses and mass-society as explanatory causes of the crisis of liberalism. The third part takes a look at the attempted offensive of the radical right to develop a political model explicitly opposed to the individualism of liberalism and the collectivism of socialism, powerfully affirming the masses as the premier political subject. The fourth part continues with this strand, turning to the German jurist Carl Schmitt whose thought consummates a long line of both scholarly and political attempts to come to terms with mass society. And, finally, we conclude by discussing how liberalism went from being a self-evidently good idea among the leading classes of Europe to become a sign and symptom of decay.

5. Holmes, *Passions and Constraint*; Freeden, *Ideologies and Political Theory*, part 2.

The divided liberalism of the 19th century

The 19th century can justly be termed the "Age of Divided Liberalism." John Stuart Mill spoke of despotic control exercised over uncivilized peoples in the colonies,[6] and the same paternalistic thinking ruled in Great Britain concerning the Irish, the working classes, and women. This has often been interpreted as hypocrisy or proof of the truly class-based nature of liberalism. To some degree this is true, but it is worth noting that liberalism always, as the Australian social scientist Barry Hindess writes, "distinguishes between what can be governed through the promotion of liberty and what must be governed in other ways."[7]

The American political philosopher Michael Walzer writes that, liberals "preached and practiced an art of separation. They drew lines, marked off different realms . . . Liberalism is a world of walls, and each one creates a new liberty."[8] It is true that liberalism is an art of separation and that every separation creates a new liberty, but it is equally essential that when a free region of liberty is created on one side of the wall, a place that is governed differently, e.g., through trust, intimacy, private property, violence, paternalism, or something else, is created on the other side.

For many liberals, there was a temporal element here that promised to dissolve or at least soften the difference, namely that in the course of time, freedom could also be extended to include the uncivilized peoples and the ordinary population at home if these people were educated and civilized. Representative or parliamentary democracy was (is?) the divided liberalism's version of democracy where population groups were progressively included and brought under control, where participation was effectively limited to voting and where what was to be governed could be constitutionally defined and clearly delimited.[9]

The rise of organized labor and popular suffrage movements can reasonably be said to have been driven by the demand for a kind of fulfillment of liberalism, but for many liberals, the time for such had not yet come and the consequences were too terrifying.[10] The fear was that liberty would be menaced if parts of the population and social groups who had previously

6. Mill, *On Liberty*, 224; Mill, *Considerations on Representative Government*, 563.

7. Hindess, "Liberalism—what's in a name?," 30.

8. Walzer, "Liberalism and the Art of Separation," 315.

9. Macpherson, *The Life and Time of Liberal Democracy*, chapter 2; Arblaster, *The Rise and Decline of Western Liberalism*, chapter 15; Holden, *Understanding Liberal Democracy*.

10. Dangerfield, *The Strange Death of Liberal England*.

been illiberally governed should henceforth be organized according to the principle of freedom. In contrast to those groups or areas that, in principle, could in the course of time be ruled in freedom, there were other areas, such as the internal operations of firms and families, or foreign policy which had to continue being ruled through other principles than freedom. Here, the fear was that the growing politicization of new social groups would create divisions between what could be governed through freedom and that which could only later—if ever and only under duress—be subjected to the same principle, and thus extending it to the entire society, meaning that liberalizing society would lead to illiberal results.

The liberal fear at the turn of the century can thus be summarized by saying that the dynamics of those forces liberated by the liberal society threatened to grow in such a way and force that they could overwhelm the very principles that brought them forth. The divided liberalism was a threat to a governable and gradual liberation. A prominent and slightly earlier proponent of this line of thinking was Alexis de Tocqueville who, frightened by the early signs of mass society in the February Revolution of 1848, shifted from a cautious liberalism viewing a general leveling as an inevitable process to a conservative position seeking to halt and contain developments that had already begun.[11]

Many liberals posed themselves questions such as those set forth in a book on liberalism in 1911, by the liberal politician and sociologist Leonard T. Hobhouse:

> Does scope for individual development, for example, consort with the idea of equality? Is popular sovereignty a practicable basis of personal freedom, or does it open an avenue to the tyranny of the mob? Will the sentiment of nationality dwell in unison with the ideal of peace? Is the love of liberty compatible with the full realization of the common will?[12]

Equality, popular sovereignty, nationalism, and commonwealth were the themes and concepts of the 19th century, but they were also far more acute in the early 20th century as some of the concepts and worries of the emerging mass society.

Hobhouse also wrote of old 19th century liberalism as "an extinct form, a fossil that occupied . . . an awkward position between two very active and energetically moving grindstones—the upper grindstone of

11. Kahan, *Aristocratic Liberalism*.
12. Hobhouse, *Liberalism*, 74.

plutocratic imperialism, and the nether grindstone of social democracy."[13] He thus advocated a new liberalism rejecting imperialism while reconciling itself with new socialist and democratic forces. He foresaw an English liberalism "free from the shackles of an individualist conception of Liberty and paving the way for the legislation of our time."[14] However, this optimism was not shared on the continent and developments in the two decades following the appearance of his book did not offer any grounds for optimism on behalf of liberalism.

The rise of mass society

In 1913, the British historian John Neville Figgis wrote that "the battle for freedom in this century is the battle of small societies to maintain their inherent life against the all-devouring Leviathan of the whole."[15] This Leviathan was obviously the state, but in a broader sense, it also designated the collectivist understanding of the social aiming to bring concepts and practices to the level of the new reality of mass society. In Oswald Spengler's *Untergang des Abendlandes* from 1917, the era is described as the "Age of the Conflict of Giants" where politics is a continuous "war without war, a war where one overbids the other in armaments and readiness to fight, a war of numbers, speed and technology."[16]

At the time, many shared a new feeling of Faustian powers. In 1909, Filippo Marinetti wrote the futurist manifesto celebrating the "beauty of speed," speed as a new condition.[17] And precisely futurism with its simultaneous enthusiasm for creation and destruction, its links to artistic creativity, but later also to fascism, its coupling of progress and war, reveals the ambivalence of development. On the one hand, we see Henry Ford's talk of "human mastery of the environment"[18] as a consequence of new technological and organizational achievements, which his own name came to symbolize, along with that of Frederick Taylor. On the other hand, however, this liberation of powers threatened to undermine, or rather explode, the basic social principles that had hitherto dominated. The writings of the

13. Ibid., 110.

14. Ibid., 112.

15. Müller, *Contesting Democracy*, 51.

16. Spengler, *Der Untergang des Abendlandes*, 1081, 1098.

17. Marinetti, "The Futurist Manifesto."

18. Ford, *My Philosophy of Industry*.

day reveal a clear ambivalence about where releasing the potential, magnifying the social and economic forces to an enormity, would end. Could the political elites control this development, or was it a development now outside of control heading for a great crash and a new (dis)order? What are, many asked nervously, the consequences of mass society?

Thoughts about mass society in this period can be said to comprise three concepts or phenomena: masses, elites, and bureaucracy whereof we will concentrate on the first two. Theories of elites, such as those formulated by, i.a., the Italians Vilfredo Pareto and Gaetano Mosca, were in many ways a kind of "sedation philosophy." The basic idea was that at all times and places society is divided into a ruling elite and a governed populace. Elite theory was an attempt to render the frightening new situation scientifically comprehensible, investigating its causes and laws. This could serve to relieve those who perceived the emergence of the masses as equivalent to chaos and disorder. The probable result of a mass society would be the reconstitution of the elite/masses relationship, and not its dissolution in "pure democracy."

Theories of the elite partly offered a reassurance of verticality and the constancy of authoritarian governance but also an exegesis of the development of history as one where elites alternate, persist but alternate. Socialism, equality, and democracy are thus impossible to accomplish. One aspect that makes the theories of the elites interesting in the context of this chapter is that it represents a sociological update of earlier conceptions of the elite with respect to mass society. In contrast to restorative conservatism, it lacks conceptions of how the old elites could maintain their hold on power in the mass societies of the democratic era, but there is also confidence that the new collectivistic powers would re-establish the eternally valid relation between the rulers and the ruled. Reality will discipline the new powers. Mass society will find its order and its leaders.

For the free-market liberal Pareto, in 1901 there was no doubt that the victory of socialism is "most probable and almost inevitable."[19] This was not due merely to developments in a progressively more interventionist state (a kind of "bourgeois socialism") that used the state to protect particular industries and interests. There was also the suicidal tendency of the liberal elites at that time: "The bourgeoisie resigns itself and remains silent." The liberal elite degenerates, it "becomes softer, milder, more humane" and, therefore, "less apt to defend its own power."[20] The new socialistic elite,

19. Pareto, *The Rise and Fall of the Elites*, 36.
20. Ibid., 62 and 59.

on the other hand, "is full of vigor and strength—the old is worked out; the new elite, bold and courageous, proclaims 'the class struggle,'—the old one childishly praises 'solidarity.' It bows its head under the blows and says thank you, instead of paying back in kind."[21]

In 1908, Mosca entered the Italian lower house as a liberal-conservative deputy. Twelve years earlier, in 1896, he had published his work, *The Ruling Class*, with a second edition in 1923. He divided the social into "a class that rules and a class that is ruled."[22] Pareto invoked the inevitability of socialism, but Mosca was doubtful; yet Mosca shared the gloomy interpretation of liberalism. According to Mosca, liberalism has had a "more brilliant record than the autocratic principle, but it is certainly a shorter record and it is less widespread over the world's surface and through history." It is primarily defined as a system where "the law is based upon the consent of the majority of the citizens, though only a small fraction of the inhabitants may be citizens" represented in a law-giving assembly—that is, the 'divided liberalism' noted above—and "the state customarily recognizes certain limits to its powers in its relations to individual citizens and to associations of citizens."[23]

In Mosca's view, however, at the close of the 19th and the beginning of the 20th century, liberalism was under pressure from its own doctrines to introduce universal suffrage, "including the illiterate, who in some countries still form a considerable percentage of the population."[24] At first, this development was governable, but Mosca apparently mistrusted the capacity of the liberal elite to maintain its monopoly on power should the concession of political equality lead to demands for economic equality, an equality that Mosca viewed as unattainable but that could nevertheless play a role, mostly a destructive role, in the future. He ended up placing his hopes in patriotism as an anti-socialist power that "has been left as the chief factor of moral and intellectual cohesion within the various countries of Europe."[25] However, when the fascists came to power in Italy, forcefully placing patriotism against socialism, Mosca withdrew from public life to teach and study, dying before the war was over.

21. Ibid., 82.
22. Mosca, *The Ruling Elite*, 50.
23. Ibid., 409. See also 398.
24. Ibid., 471.
25. Ibid., 482.

The one who contributed most to explain the leftist parties' inevitable restoration of inequality between the elite and the masses, was Robert Michels, a German sociologist and socialist (later allied with the Italian syndicalists and even fascists)[26] whose book on the oligarchic tendencies of political parties dates to 1911. Mass society has changed the party from a loose association of free spirits to "a fighting organization in the political sense of the term, and must as such conform to the laws of tactics."[27] According to Michels, the modern party is one of the expressions of increasing bureaucratization, and it will inevitably be organized as an oligarchy reproducing the inequality of the elite/masses relationship internally within the party—also within socialist parties where the explicit policies support the diametrically opposed. For Michels, in the future, power would belong to the socialists, but it would be an elite society all the same.

One of these signs calls to mind Pareto's observation that the liberal elite had given up the fight. In a chapter entitled "The Class Struggle and its Disintegrating Influence upon the Bourgeoisie," Michels notes the large number of socialist leaders with bourgeois backgrounds, meaning that the liberal bourgeoisie was not defending itself but was rather seeing a desertion to another class and another social principle, concluding: "We may regard it as an established historical law that races, legal systems, institutions, and social classes, are inevitably doomed to destruction from the moment they or those who represent them have lost faith in the future."[28]

In his famous 1919 lecture on "Politics as a profession," Max Weber made the following observation about the development from that which we can call the liberal parliamentary era to the modern age of mass democracy:

> Now then, the most modern forms of party organizations stand in sharp contrast to this idyllic state in which circles of notables and, above all, members of parliament rule. These modern forms are the children of democracy, of mass franchise, of the necessity to woo and organize the masses, and develop the utmost unity of direction and the strictest discipline.[29]

Weber said that the time of the independent politician who was free by virtue of their own means and abilities was over. The age of the paid professional had arrived. With increasing desperation, Weber tried to find a

26. Beetham, "From Socialism to Fascism."
27. Michels, *Political Parties*, 78.
28. Ibid., 233.
29. Weber, "Politics as Vocation," 102.

popularly acceptable, plebiscitary, answer to the disintegrative tendencies of mass society. He wished to unify two tendencies that would otherwise be mutually incompatible, namely Caesarian charisma and parliamentary conventionalism. Parliament should henceforth serve as a place for upbringing and disciplining strong leaders who could supplement parliament's proper bureaucratic, objective and procedural process of law-making (legal sovereignty) with charismatic legitimacy. At the same time (one would hope that), the parliamentary process would prevent a "parliamentary Caesar" who could transform himself into a real despot.[30] Thus, could parliamentary legitimacy—the only system of governance with legitimacy in a democracy—be preserved while also accommodating the requirements of efficiency and leadership required in a complex mass society. And it would be achieved precisely through a transformation of parliament from a deliberative assembly of the few who should control power to an acclaiming assembly of the masses who should produce the rulers.

The theories of the elite were concerned with the masses: there thus rose psychological and cultural theories of the masses to join the sociological theories of the elite. The political dimension of theories of the masses is a conception of a shift of the relevant political subject from the educated individual to the uneducated masses. Probably the most familiar theoretician of the masses was the French scholar Gustave Le Bon, who drafted a theory of the masses in *Psychologie des foules* (1895). The work influenced, i.a., Mussolini and Sigmund Freud, as well as Freud's nephew Edward Bernays, who in the book *Propaganda* (1928) used the theories to develop PR-techniques. Le Bon's basic thesis was that his own age was characterized by two tectonic shifts: "The first is the destruction of those religious, political, and social beliefs in which all the elements of our civilization are rooted. The second is the creation of entirely new conditions of existence and thought as the result of modern scientific and industrial discoveries."[31] An exhaustion of the ideas and ideals of the 19th century has set in:

> On the ruins of so many ideas formerly considered beyond discussion, and to-day decayed or decaying, of so many sources of authority that successive revolutions have destroyed, this power, which alone has arisen in their stead, seems soon destined to absorb the others. While all our ancient beliefs are tottering and

30. Weber, "Parliament und Regierung." See also Baehr, "Max Weber and the Avatars of Caesarism."

31. Le Bon, *The Crowd*, ix–x.

disappearing, while the old pillars of society are giving way one by one, the power of the crowd is the only force that nothing menaces, and of which the prestige is continually on the increase. The age we are about to enter will in truth be the ERA OF CROWDS.[32]

According to Le Bon, society is no longer guided by the elite, but rather by an unqualified mob. The soul of the masses is now the driving element in politics and not rational deliberation. It is "the philosophy of number,"[33] which determines the course of history. Seeing that liberalism fits a bygone era, it is not an irrelevant idea and practice to consider. In its place, socialism has emerged. It addresses the mass soul directly, expresses its desires and hatreds, especially its resentment toward the wealthy. Through socialism the masses can exercise their destructive impulses. Happily, Le Bon (in a very misogynistic and racist use of language) saw clear signs that the masses also wished to be ruled and to obey, which rendered mass psychology the contemporary means of political control of the age. What he suggested was a total manipulation with the newest sociological and psychological tools for an emergent mass society.

Less oriented toward the practical rule of the masses and more concerned with the cultural implications of the phenomenon is the other of the great mass society treatises of the period, *La Rebelión de las Masas* (1931) by the Spanish liberal philosopher José Ortega y Gasset. The *Revolt of the Masses* was his concept for the relationship that "the ordinary man, hitherto guided by others, has resolved to govern the world himself." This is a "rebellion against [the masses'] own destiny"—which is to be led.[34] What rules now is what he termed a hyperdemocracy, "in which the mass acts directly, outside the law, imposing its aspirations and its desires by means of material pressure."[35] The masses wish to act themselves, non-deliberative, a-rational, directly, letting the force of reason be replaced by the material pressure of sheer numbers. The masses no longer select representatives. Now, "the mass believes that it has the right to impose and to give force of law to notions born in the café."[36]

According to Ortega y Gasset, liberalism was "the prototype of indirect action," where "the public authority, in spite of being all-powerful,

32. Ibid., x.

33. Ibid., xiii.

34. Ortega y Gasset, *The Revolt of the Masses*, 97 and 116.

35. Ibid., 17.

36. Ibid., 17-18.

limits itself." It leaves open a space "for those to who neither think nor feel as it does." Liberalism is "the supreme form of generosity; it is the right which the majority concedes to minorities and hence it is the noblest cry that has ever resounded in this planet."[37] This voice has been reduced to silence, however, by the howling masses. They march into politics through direct action and accept no dissent. The mass "is the norm which proposes the annulment of all norms, which suppresses all intermediate process between our purpose and its execution. It is the Magna Carta of barbarism."[38]

The English social scientist Richard Bellamy notes that even though these theoretical developments expressed a common European experience, there are also national variations so that to a certain degree one can assert that: (1) the theory of the masses was a French reaction to the tendency of its revolutionary tradition to take to the streets; (2) the theory of the elites was an Italian reaction to clientele politics under pressure; and (3) the bureaucratic and organizational theory was a German reaction to the increase of the reliance on technical means in the state, the parties and the firms.[39] Common to all is the idea of a transition from individualism to collectivism.

This new collectivist train of thought found many forms of political expression. Two of them are expressed among the Social Democrats and the Bolsheviks, respectively. In the program of the Danish Social Democrats from February 1913, they speak of "eliminating capitalist private ownership of the means of production, to change it into a socialist common ownership and to organize the workers to take over and manage production in the socialist society."[40] Among the Bolsheviks, it was Lenin who was inspired by Ford and Taylor as he summarized the logic of the masses in 1920: "Communism is the power of the councils and electrification of the entire land." While it was the dominant understanding among many, both socialist and non-socialist at the beginning of the century—and perhaps indeed all the way to the 1920s—that the future belonged to socialism, more and more non-socialists began to look for other non-socialist mass society alternatives.

37. Ibid., 76.
38. Ibid., 75.
39. Bellamy, "The advent of the masses."
40. Socialdemokratiet, "Program for det danske Socialdemokrati," 10.

"The total" as a counter-principle to "the liberal"

Réflexions sur la violence (1908, English translation 1914) by the French philosopher Georges Sorel is a potent example of the search for alternatives to liberalism. He wrote that "there are no longer any Liberal convictions, since the Liberals have ceased to be animated by their former warlike passions."[41] With the leading ideology of the 19th century hollowed out, what was to take its place? For Sorel, at various different points, this was Bolshevism, syndicalism, and fascism, and these possibilities spell out quite clearly the dominating impression from the mid-1920s onwards that there was no longer the socialist possibility alone.

At the end of the 1920s and the beginning of the 1930s, the idea that the liberal age was over formed the background for a radicalization of conceptions, most prominently around "the total" as the principle opposing "the liberal." The age of individual freedom was over. At the extreme right—but this extended even to liberal and social democratic circles—the fear was that only communism had developed a party organization and ideology suited to the new age. "The total" became the common designation for a proposed organizational principle for mass society that sought to take over from liberalism and as such face communism on its own terrain. Fascism and Nazism emerged partly as counter ideologies and partly as propositions for the solution of mass society.

In Germany, General Erich von Ludendorff spoke of "Total War,"[42] the writer Ernst Jünger wrote about "Total Mobilization,"[43] the jurist Ernst Forsthoff evoked the "Total State,"[44] and in 1939 the Nazi-leader Joseph Goebbels spoke of "The Total Revolution of National Socialism," expressing himself thus: "The revolution we have carried out is a total one. It has embraced all areas of public life and transformed them from below. It has completely changed and recast the relationship of people to each other, to the state, and to life itself."[45]

In Spain, the creator of the fascist-inspired Falage Española party, José Antonio Primo de Rivera, spoke of the need for "a total feeling for the Fatherland, for life, for History, and it is that total feeling, clear not on paper but in the soul, which will tell us in every concrete situation what we

41. Sorel, *Reflections on Violence*, 210-211.
42. Ludendorff, *Der totale Krieg*.
43. Jünger, "Die totale Mobilmachung."
44. Forsthoff, *Der Totale Staat*.
45. Goebbels, "The Total Revolution of National Socialism."

must do and what we must prefer."[46] The concept of "the total" clearly corresponded to a contemporary experience while also containing a promise of the future.

This we can clearly see expressed in the formation of the essence of the right-wing in the early interwar period. Italian fascism attracted a great deal of attention across Europe as an authoritarian answer to mass society and a counter-response to socialism. There are thus good reasons for taking a closer look at the court philosopher of fascism, Giovanni Gentile, and how he arranged the relationship between the liberalism of the past and the fascism of the future, taking "the total" as his basic starting point.

Gentile was a philosopher and classic 19th century liberal. However, in 1923, he became the Minister of Education in Mussolini's government, and at the very start, described his support for fascism as the last chance for saving Italy from socialism. He held various prominent positions in the fascist government and was a member of the Saló-republic of 1943 until shot by anti-fascist partisans on April 15, 1944. In 1925, he organized a conference for fascist culture with the aim of binding the Italian intelligentsia to fascism. At the end of the conference, Gentile wrote the "Manifesto for fascist intellectuals" presenting fascism's assumption of power as a spiritual awakening of the Italian nation created "when a band of men, returned from the trenches and resolved to fight vigorously against the demo-socialist politics that then prevailed, gathered around Benito Mussolini." Fascist violence is presented as "breaking the law in order to set up a new law, a force armed against the State to establish the new State." And the state against which the fascists had fought and overthrew was "liberal, but its liberalism was the agnostic and acquiescent kind that understands only external freedom—the State which is liberal because it remains outside the free citizen's mind as if it were a mechanical system apart from the activity of each individual."[47]

According to Gentile, the liberal state was thus characterized and thus wrong in that it assumed and maintained a difference between the state and the individual. This is exactly the difference or separation that fascism rejected and fought. This becomes clear in a 1925 text, "What is Fascism?," where the age of individualism (The Renaissance) is equated with:

> indifference, skepticism, and distracted cynicism of those who
> have nothing to defend, not in their family, their Fatherland, or

46. Rivera, "Total feeling."
47. Gentile, "Manifesto of the Fascist Intellectuals."

in the world where every human personality conscious of its own value and personal dignity invests itself. The Italians of the period had nothing to defend because they did not believe in anything beyond the free and pleasurable play of their own creative fantasy. From thence, came the frivolity of a pattern of behavior both decadent and corrupt. That behavior slowly extinguished the active sentiment of nationality and thereby enfeebled souls.[48]

According to Gentile, the liberal has thus always, even under Mazzini, weakened the state because they "gave the individual priority before all else. We still have those liberals underfoot who prove recalcitrant, and resist the irresistible movement of history."[49] Fascism battles liberal individualism, its state/person-dualism and its understanding of freedom as the individual's freedom from the state: "Today we affirm liberty—but within the State. The State is the nation, that nation that appears as something that limits us and subordinates us, and makes us sense and think and speak, and more than anything else, to *be* in a certain manner."[50] The state is thus neither neutral nor external with respect to its inhabitants. On the contrary, it is an ethical state: "The Fascist ethical State, it must be recognized, is no longer the agnostic State of the old liberalism. Its ethical form is spiritual; its personality is cognizant; its system is will."[51]

Fascism is thus "a total conception of life,"[52] including all the circumstances of life, making these the obligations of the state to such a degree that according to Gentile there could not be a meaningful distinction between the state and individual—but with the decisive addition that it is the state that molds and transforms the individual. Liberalism seeks "a liberty in itself, that confronts the State. It wants a liberty that is the limit of the State, resigning itself to a belief that the State is the (unfortunately inevitable) limit of liberty." The hallmark of fascism, on the contrary, is that it "courageously and vigorously opposed itself to the prejudices of contemporary liberalism—to affirm that the liberty protected by liberalism serves neither

48. Gentile, "What is Fascism?," 44.
49. Ibid., 46.
50. Ibid., 47.
51. Ibid., 55.
52. Ibid., 57.

the people nor the individual."[53] The fascist state is "an authoritarian state that does not accept the anarchic liberalism of the individualist."[54]

Liberalism is portrayed here as counter-national, counter-state, and counter-mass in its celebration of rights and hedonism rather than duty and sacrifice. It does not fit the new realities of Italy or Europe. Following Gentile, fascism was the only possibility for Italy to become modern and nationalistic. As he writes in a 1928 article in *Foreign Affairs*, explaining fascism to an American public: "Fascism came into being to meet serious problems of politics in post-war Italy."[55] In contrast to liberalism's splitting of society into autonomous units with its preferences for the individual over the collective, Gentile assumed that one had to understand "the comprehensive, or as Fascists say, the "totalitarian" scope of its doctrine, which concerns itself not only with political organization and political tendency, but with the whole will and thought and feeling of the nation."[56] The practical implications of "the total" is here "the totalitarian."

The official exegesis of fascism, "The Doctrine of Fascism" (1932) was originally published under Mussolini's name but written by Gentile, and it is here that we finally find the real quintessence of fascism's understanding of liberalism as both a problematic and outmoded doctrine. Fascism is "opposed to classical liberalism which arose as a reaction to absolutism and exhausted its historical function when the State became the expression of the conscience and will of the people. Liberalism denied the State in the name of the individual; Fascism reasserts." Liberalism is "the historic and logical anteroom to anarchy," and it is now going about "preparing to close the doors of its temples, deserted by the peoples who feel that the agnosticism it professed in the sphere of economics and the indifferentism of which it has given proof in the sphere of politics and morals, would lead the world to ruin in the future as they have done in the past." The conclusion on this as on the other "total" criticisms of liberalism is that "all the political experiments of our day are anti-liberal." The counter-practice to liberalism is the fascism that "interprets, develops, and potentates the whole life of a people," described as totalitarianism.[57]

53. Gentile, "Origins and Doctrine of Fascism," 30–31.
54. Ibid., 35.
55. Ibid., 301.
56. Ibid., 299.
57. Gentile, "The Doctrine of Fascism."

IV. Carl Schmitt

One of the most important European interpreters of "the total" and its immanent criticism of liberalism was the German jurist Carl Schmitt whose work summarized and radicalized the thoughts of the era about masses (Sorel, le Bon), bureaucracy (Weber), elites (Pareto, Michels), the total (Ludendorff, Forsthoff, Jünger), and their shared fears of communism. His life and work points toward the total-thought scheme culminating in Nazi totalitarianism.

According to Schmitt, liberalism is characterized by a constant flight from the political. He denounced the goals and program of liberalism as ambitions that "now there should only be organizational-technical or economic-sociological tasks and no longer political problems."[58] From this follows one of Schmitt's main points in criticizing the liberals specifically and modernity in general: the impossibility of shifting political conflict into neutral spheres. Liberalism transforms the enemy into a competitor in the economic realm and into a discussion partner in parliament. Liberalism is, Schmitt says, characterized by a constant striving at *depoliticization* with political decisions shifted to economics, technology, morals, etc. where it is expected that things will spontaneously self-organize without difficulties or need of decisions or politics.

In liberal society, the individual and his or her liberty are the highest categories. This means that all moral categories and imperatives must be dissolved in order not to stand in the way of the individual's freedom of action. According to Schmitt, the liberal is, moreover, characterized by a distance to the real, as reality cannot be permitted to intrude in such a commanding way that it obliges the individual to make decisions and take actions. The possibilities must always remain open and undecided. The liberal principle of action is thus passivity and the endless postponement of decisions. Instead, the liberal indulges himself in 'eternal discussions,' which was Schmitt's designation for the 'political' position of the liberals. For Schmitt, politics is characterized by either/or situations demanding clear and final decisions. The liberals are bad administrators of the affairs of the state that ultimately deal with actions and decisions related to survival.

According to Schmitt, the liberal constitutional state operates on the basis of an insubstantial and value-free functionalism. The parliamentary law-lawmaker is indifferent with regard to the content of the law enacted. Neutrality is first and foremost a neutrality that is between right and wrong.

58. Schmitt, *Politische Theologie*, 82.

The parliamentary liberal constitutional state does not have any immanent or inviolable values, only inviolable procedures. Where these are fulfilled, the law is legal. This principle opens and eases access to political power and is an essential characteristic of the liberal constitutional state. No actor may take power legally and then hinder other actors assuming power. The equality of opportunity must remain open or the parliamentary law making state loses its rationale. This means that the liberal constitutional state is defenseless in the face of the enemies within.

Schmitt went on to write that the assumptions for neutrality were initially that the liberal state still maintained bits of the non- and pre-liberal states, namely the executive decisional capabilities of the absolutist state along with its military and civil service. The second assumption was that society consisted of isolated individuals and loosely joined parties that were "hardly firm or established, rather fluid or airy,"[59] to the degree that they were nearly non-existent. The third assumption was the non-existence of a socially organized opposition to liberal society. For Schmitt, 1848 is the year "when socialism reached a politically important size such that it could hope one day to realize its ideas."[60] In Schmitt's interpretation, 1848 marks the arrival of the masses in politics. The neutral liberal state is now torn to pieces by the extension of the franchise, by the inclusion of the masses and its demands into the political decision-making apparatus.

In Schmitt's view, liberal ideas and institutions are not suitable for mass democracy since they assume another social order. It uses instruments that served well in the age of education and property (*Bildung und Besitz*), but threaten the dissolution of the state when the masses are organized to enforce their demands. The rise of mass democracy developed political bonds that are far from those of the liberal ideal of loosely linked individuals. These have become total parties, mobilizing armies of professional politicians and party foot-soldiers who take control of the formation of will. The 'total parties' transform the voters into clients and represent their interests from cradle to grave. The parties have shifted their character from being discussion clubs to those of the Weimar Republic that included armed self-defense groups. Loyalties had switched from the state to the party. The pluralization of loyalty illustrates the parties' erosion of the prerogatives of the state and the reduction of the state to an instrument for the conquest of power and the fulfilment of special interests.

59. Schmitt, *Hüter der Verfassung*, 83.
60. Schmitt, *Geistesgeschichtliche Lage*, 65.

The liberal depoliticization of the state paradoxically leads to an over-politicization. Since the state has lost its capacity and will to define the political, masses of special interests move into the domain of the state and try to redefine the political so that it is literally transformed into their own demands and image of the world. The state becomes the special interest organization of society. When society moves into the state, this leads to the functional de-differentiation of state and society, and everything becomes potentially political. "Society becomes the state, as the state becomes a business-state, a culture-state, a caretaker-state, a welfare-state, a provider-state."[61] The now overburdened state is reduced to a reflection of the pluralistically divided society: "When the 'earthly god' falls from his throne, the parties slaughter the mighty Leviathan and every one cuts his own piece of meat from its body."[62]

The predominant theme in the preceding paragraphs was the incapacity of the liberal constitutional state to deal with mass democracy in an economic-technical age. The conception of the state, with its principles and instruments, became anachronistic and lacked the capacity to function or adapt to the new age. According to Schmitt, the intellectual climate in Europe continued to suffer from outdated liberal conceptions. Beyond that, the liberal leadership was neither mentally nor conceptually suited to political leadership since it confused neutrality with leadership. The analysis suggested to him that a governmental authority of command freed from the constitutional and parliamentary bonds and outfitted with massive means of power would put the state in a position to assert itself once again above and opposite society.

The state must assert its primacy. The state only appears and acts as a state when it undertakes leadership, subordinates the new means of mass politics to its will, rather than letting itself be subdued by them. If the political powers renounce these new means of power on the basis of moral prejudices or liberal feelings, other actors with more will power will use them to take on executive powers and become the state. The state, Schmitt says, is basically whoever manages "to conquer all the means of power needed for political sovereignty. That it does so is the sure sign that it really is a state."[63] That kind of state is total by virtue of its quality and energy. It is in Schmitt's words a qualitative total state. It is total in setting its own goals and policies,

61. Schmitt, *Hüter der Verfassung*, 62.

62. Schmitt, "Staatsethik," 152.

63. Schmitt, "Weiterentwicklung des totalen Staats," 212.

in its own decision to act and intervene, or not, and in its commandment of the new means of power. Refusing the new means of power is the refusal of political leadership, subordinating itself to a stronger political power. The qualitatively total state exhibits strength in its rejection of neutrality and "equal chances" in the face of its enemies: "Inside such a state no state enemies, state inhibiting or divisive forces are allowed to emerge. It does not think about handing over the new means of power to its enemies and destroyers or to let itself be undermined by any slogans, liberalism, rule of law, or whatever."[64] Any political elite must seize the necessary technical and propagandistic measures to strengthen the state:

> Every state must take hold of the new technical means, film and ra-
> dio. No state, however liberal, exists, which will not claim for itself
> the control of an intensive censorship and control of film and radio.
> No state can permit itself to surrender to others these new techni-
> cal means of information, mass influence, mass suggestion, and the
> construction of a 'public,' or more correctly: collective opinion.[65]

Schmitt diagnosed the technological age's shift from the formation of popular opinion as going from parliamentary discussions out into society and the then new situation where centralized mass media had direct influence on public opinion. The political elite must choose one of two ways in regard to these new powerful tools: "either renounce the liberal conceptions of freedom from yesteryear or renounce a decisive aspect of its power, and thereby its political existence."[66] Renounce the liberal freedoms and principles, Schmitt says, or perish under the threat of mass society and mass parties.

The Italian fascist state did just that, liberated itself from the liberal ideas of autonomous organization and exercised political leadership. According to Schmitt, fascism recognized the new social, economic, military, and communicative reality—and drew the necessary political consequences. Through its strong will and the exploitations of a national mythology, Italy reasserted the state above and beyond the economic and social conflicts of interest and reaffirmed the primacy of the state. Italy had effectively defeated proletarian communism and liberal neutralism. This analysis of totalitarianism's will to statehood is an essential part of the explanation for Schmitt's 'conversion' to Nazism after January 1933. As he wrote in 1934: "Today, when the concrete order-thinking again lives with help from a new

64. Ibid., 213.
65. Ibid., 212.
66. Schmitt, "Machtpositionen des modernen Staates," 368–69.

fellowship, the judicial axiom that fidelity, discipline and honor shall not be distinguished from leadership, is more obviously true than an outdated individualism of the liberal constitutional state with its division of power and normative way of thinking."[67]

Conclusion

"The politics of the future are social politics."[68] This is what the liberal statesman Joseph Chamberlain said in 1883. By this, he meant that the hub of politics had shifted from individual freedom to the welfare of the people. This shift was a great challenge for the liberals. As the state and its interventions grew, the demands of the populace grew from day to day; new groups with new expectations established themselves and raised their voice. One group of liberals remained true to the classic 19th century *laissez-faire* liberalism, which understood the contradiction between freedom and state as fundamental. Another group, e.g., Hobhouse and Keynes stood for a new liberalism, a social liberalism, using the state and social policy to advance freedom. Other liberals, e.g., Weber, "solved" the problem by adding a nationalist dimension to their liberalism, and later, as noted briefly hereinabove, a Caesaristic mechanism to use democratic legitimacy against real democratic results. Others left liberalism in favor of the new ideologies, particularly fascism and Nazism (and in the post-war the Italian and German Christian-Democratic teaching).[69]

If a single formula can be applied to the 20th century, it is the century of the state, the only form of organization that can direct mass society. On the continent, in particular, there was other social and political forces that forcefully explored and molded politics for mass society; forces that did not have the liberal's limitation grounded in a fear of the state. Rather than viewing the state as an obstacle or force of resistance, they understood the state as an ally or instrument in political struggle. This state-orientation was very diverse and reaches from, e.g., the social democrats and conservatives to the communists and Nazis, of whom it can be said that they absorbed the social question much more thoroughly than most liberals of the age did. The interwar period did not see the end of liberalism but it brought to a close every political ideology that did not integrate the state and the masses

67. Schmitt, Über die drei Arten," 52.

68. Arblaster, *The Rise and Decline*, 284.

69. Müller, *Contesting Democracy*, chapter 4.

into the heart of its thought. The Nazi-German and Russian-Bolshevik answer was "the total," not least the internal total war discussed in the next chapter. The post-war West-European answer became the welfare state.

"The total" is a will to state power and political action. It became the language of a political will liberated from constitutionalism and moral limitations; free to reshape itself, its social environment and each and every individual; self-consciously transgressing the public/private divide from the standpoint of the state; openly subordinating the individual the collective or state imperative; and celebrating a notion of politics as war, a "total war" fought at all times, internally and externally; basically, an idea that life, individually and collectively, is reducible to existential warfare. Totalitarianism emerged as the practical answer to the total challenges of the mass society. Once that desire for a total reorganization was formulated, and a state was seized to implement it, the total enemy could also be formulated and fought. When one is in a "total revolution," only a total enemy will do.

4

Totalitarian Enmity: Understanding the Total Enemy through Schmitt, Arendt, Foucault, and Agamben

During the Stalin era, a Cheka deputy, M. Latsis, said: "Do not look for evidence that the accused rose up against Soviet power with arms or with words. The first thing you should ask is to which class he belongs, his social origin, his education, and his profession. It is these questions that should decide his fate. This is the essence of Red Terror."[1] When, after the end of the Nazi regime, a doctor who participated in the mass killings was asked how he could reconcile the Hippocratic Oath with his actions during the war, the doctor replied: "Of course I am a doctor and I want to preserve life. And out of respect for human life, I would remove a gangrenous appendix from a diseased body. The Jew is the gangrenous appendix in the body of mankind."[2]

How are we to understand two such radical statements on the enemy? This article will explore the idea that totalitarianism introduced a completely new and hitherto unseen enmification process and enemy category, namely the "total enemy" whose status was derived from being rather than action. Rather than focus on totalitarian actors or enmification processes, this article will reconstruct how a number of significant thinkers have tried

---

1. Gregory, *Terror by Quota*, 110.
2. Lifton, *The Nazi Doctors*, 15–16.

to grasp and conceptualize this "break" in the history of enmity introduced by totalitarianism.

The article presents three main sections, starting with Carl Schmitt and his interwar theories of "the total" as a new political and ideational armament of the state as well as his post-war reflections on the "absolute enemy." The second section follows with Hannah Arendt's elaborate but unsystematized theory of the totalitarian enemy and her strong thesis of a completely new enemy complex in totalitarian societies. This section will also include Zygmunt Bauman's theory of the Holocaust and the idea that in racism one "exists before one acts" making one's qualification as an enemy something one bears as a body. The first two sections point towards the third and final section, dealing with Michel Foucault's and Giorgio Agamben's notion of a bio-political enmity and totalitarianism's conflation of war/peace, exception/normality, and individual/collectivity.

Carl Schmitt's many enemies

Perhaps no one scholar has been as closely associated with enmity as Carl Schmitt. He made it a defining feature of his definition of politics; much of his work can be said to be explorations of the instrumental value of various enmity forms, while also seeing these forms as diagnostic symptoms of various political and judicial constellations. And finally, he himself, due to his involvement in Nazi politics, is the center of various enmity positions. That, however, is not our concern here; rather, it is to summarize his theory of various enemy forms and document how he—despite a 1937 article on "Total Enemy, Total War, Total State"[3]—never really engaged with the totalitarian form of enmity.

Schmitt's 1937-article was part of a broader Continental European interwar exploration of "the total," an exploration Schmitt took a very active part in. "The total" was mobilized in opposition to what was thought to be the now obsolete liberal era of individualism and non-intervention. As I discussed in chapter 3 above, in the era of planning and the masses, the concept of "the total" seemed to summarize the new political challenge. The concept of "the total" clearly resonated with a reading of the times and seemed to summarize a forceful approach to political power.

It is in this context that Schmitt wrote his 1937 article and other minor pieces on "the total," reflecting on the related developments of war, the

---

3. Schmitt, "Totaler Feind, totaler Krieg, totaler Staat."

state and enmity. They were phrased or interpreted through a competition between logics, the logic of territoriality—characterized by limits, hedging of conflicts, rational or conventional enmity—versus the logic of universality—characterized by a complete disintegration of all limits and a totalizing, all-including enmity.

Firstly, we have "conventional enmity" (or just enmity): the ideal according to which other enmities are measured. This is the great achievement of the nation state era. It is also what we here describe as political enmity. It describes a relation of enmity between states who recognize, fight and negotiate with each other. The conventional just enemy is recognized as an equal and the war is thus contained through international law and a code of honor among combatants. European international law was, according to Schmitt, based, inscribed or grounded in earth, territory, boundaries drawn on the land and, ultimately, on the division into states. From this derives the real, the contained, and the most peaceful available kind of law, war and enmity. The Europe of land-based law is the classical epoch: the era of the *jus publicum Europaeum*, where Europe writes the law. This state of (idealized) international relations is disrupted when Britain turns to the sea. A split is introduced in Europe. Law based on land develops, according to Schmitt, a codified war, a contained enmity, where state confronts state, each with a regularized army. Only the fighting armies are, in principle, enemies; the civilian population is considered beyond the fighting. This is the scene of the conventional enmity. However, once a dominant power turns to the sea, all this changes: the sea is a stateless space, which renders the interstate containment of enmity impossible.[4] Britain initiates a "space revolution" in its choice of the sea.[5]

Out of Britain's maritime dominance, an absolute enmity emerges. The sea is a natural borderland: it isn't owned by anyone; it defies proper institutionalization or demarcation; and, it evades being filled with infrastructural power. The sea resists the state. The sea, then, offers another law, another organizational, political and juridical modus operandi, which stands in direct opposition to the state or land based order. In the years 1588–1688, the island of Britain detaches itself from main*land* Europe and becomes the metropolis of an overseas world empire and the creator of the industrial revolution: all this without attaining the continental state

4. Schmitt, "Staat als ein konkreter," 382.
5. Schmitt, *Land und Meer*, 54–57.

characteristics.[6] Free trade, industry and safe passage became catchwords of a new universalist-liberal world order, which breaks down the line separating Europe from the rest of the world: a line that used to be defined according to what Schmitt considered substantial notions of similarity and equality rather than the new functionalist and internationalist notions of a single world (market).

The paradigmatic war of the state/land order is the clash on the battlefield. The paradigmatic war of the maritime order, on the other hand, is the sea war. Inherent in the two are, according to Schmitt, completely different concepts and realities of both war and enmity. In the sea war, the war effort is also directed against the trade and economics of the enemy. This makes civilians and neutrals direct participants in the war.[7] "The British sea war is total in its capacity for a total enmity. It knows, like only one of the great world historical arts of war, how to mobilize religious, ideological, psychological and moral force."[8] The war is not won through a decisive battle but by starving and exhausting the enemy: blockade, economic pressure, and sanctions. Sea war is, according to Schmitt, the first liberal war and its implicit logic is a "space-abolishing universalism,"[9] which, in Schmitt's understanding, is the first reappearance of the borderland in Europe. The British are, according to Schmitt, not even principally against exodus, against moving their nation elsewhere, which shows the same kind of lack of attachment to the land, as he thought to discover in Protestants who could erect their industry anywhere.[10] Schmitt's narrative is based on the presumption of benign limitation: that is, of the moderating effects of being embedded in a particular, limited context and the dangers of universalist disembedding.

This enmity threatens to destroy European interstate law and thereby the containment of war inherent in the paradigm. The enemy is no longer the concrete other on the battlefield but is, on the contrary, being portrayed as the enemy of humanity. As the battlefield shifts to the sea, the constraints of enmity are abolished. The sea war reintroduces the private contractor of violence, which the nation state had incorporated and conquered as a

6. Schmitt, *Hamlet oder Hekuba*, 66–67.

7. Schmitt, *Land und Meer*, 87-88; "Das Meer gegen das Land"; "Raum und Grossraum im Völkerrecht," 253–59.

8. Schmitt, "Totaler Feind, totaler Krieg, totaler Staat," 271.

9. Schmitt, "Die Raumrevolution," 390.

10. Schmitt, "Staatliche Souveränität und freies Meer," 421.

precondition for its sovereign status. Privateers, freebooters and pirates with semi-public authorization enter the war, blurring the boundary between combatant and civilian on the side of both perpetrator and victim. The former divide between enemy and criminal, combatant and civilian/neutral, war and policing, and, ultimately, between war and peace, dissolves. The enemy is criminalized, which again leads to interventions described as police actions or punitive expeditions. The legitimization of war goes from being described in terms of state interest to that of morality. The new sea-based warfare (which is, of course, also conducted on land: it's a general mode of war) requires a new concept of enmity to justify its means of combat.

This is the concept of 'enemy of humanity'; an enmity which, according to Schmitt, is logically meaningless, as humanity cannot have an enemy, as he/she/they would then be effectively non-human. The concept, however, is still very useful politically-ideologically: "'Humanity' is an especially useful ideological instrument for imperial expansions."[11] One side is prosecutor, judge and executioner, whereas the other side is "enemy and criminal, vermin and criminal."[12] A new discriminatory concept of war emerges. The concept of enemy is lifted from the concrete confrontation; the aim of the war is no longer just the defeat of a present and actual enemy; the interested parties in the conflict are no longer two or more states; the battlefield is no longer geographically contained and the duration of the war is no longer temporally contained; the war is now a just war; the enemy is a global criminal and the war aim suddenly "concerns the whole world and is of global significance: It is about naming the political opponent as a criminal who acts against the interest of the whole world and who is the last barrier before world peace."[13] To invoke humanity is to occupy a universal concept and thereby immunize one's own position and defame that of the other. Schmitt is fond of quoting Pierre-Joseph Proudhon, who allegedly said: "Whoever invokes humanity wants to cheat."[14] This change in operative enmities makes war more not less likely. It provides new possibilities for "international *hostis*-declarations" and "legitimates and sanctions some kinds of wars,"[15] namely wars couched in universalist, moralist rather than state interest terms.

11. Schmitt, *Der Begriff des Politischen*, 55.

12. Schmitt, *Glossarium*, 76.

13. Schmitt, "Strukturwandel des Internationalen Rechts," 664.

14. Schmitt, *Der Begriff des Politischen*, 55.

15. Ibid., 52, 57.

After the war, rather than reflect on the "total enemy" of the totalitarian state, Schmitt chose, on the one hand, to continue to apply the basic dichotomy between limited state wars and unlimited universalist wars and focus on a typology of enmities derived from the struggle between the state and state subversive forces: namely the partisan (real enmity) and the revolutionary (absolute enmity). These two enmities are, like the total enmity of the inter-war and war years, developed in opposition to the inter-state conventional enmity.

"Real enmity" is enmity that cannot be contained within or by international law.[16] The prime example is the partisan—a non-state contractor of violence—where the rules of law do not and cannot apply as they are characterized by the opposite of the regular army: they hide their status as combatants; they merge with the civilian population; they evade the battle; they have no clear hierarchical chain of command: "The partisan leads the regular army away from the traditional theatre of war and into a secret clandestine underground war, without traditional fronts, without emblems or uniforms."[17] Real enmity, according to Schmitt, emerges where a war is being fought by the population, or segments of it, to expel an intruder. Its first appearance was, according to Schmitt, in the opposition to Napoleon's war on Spain and Prussia. Napoleon's army can be considered the first modern army with mass mobilization, national conscription, national propaganda etc. And, at the same moment, its counter-force emerges. This shows the precarious nature of the conventional enmity, which produces its own challengers and the fight against the partisan takes on an irregular form, where the fight against the partisan entails copying his tactics. The partisan explodes the distinction between enemy and criminal. The partisan knows that his opponents consider him a criminal acting outside both juridical and moral law. The partisan, on his part, tries to gain political status as a military and political opponent: that is, to turn the real enmity into a conventional one, although his tactics consistently hinder this transformation.

"Absolute enmity" is the radicalization of real enmity. The goal is no longer concrete and limited but pervasive and universal. Whereas real enmity is carried by "freedom fighters" liberating an occupied nation, absolute enmity is carried by world-aggressive actors fighting for an abstract notion of justice. The goal is liberation of mankind. Schmitt sees this figure

16. Schmitt, *Theorie des Partisanen.*
17. Slomp, "The Theory of the Partisan," 510.

as a degeneration of the telluric partisan. The world-aggressive partisan has cut his connection to the "real," concrete fight; the local fight is only one front in a global struggle. The telluric partisan locates his enemy in a concrete geographical and historical setting, whereas the world-aggressive partisan views his enemy as a universal enemy: a class, a race, a religion. The enemy is de-humanized; he stands in the way of the final liberation and his complete destruction is hence both necessary and justified. This is a war without limitations. All containments are dissolved; all demarcations other than that between friend and enemy are meaningless.

In his diary from the years 1947–51, *Glossarium*, Schmitt explains the difference between conventional and absolute enmity by the different behavior of the German army on the Western and Eastern fronts during WW2. Against the West-European (state) enemies, Nazi-Germany fought a basically non-discriminatory war, where the rules of combat were by and large upheld and the enemy was considered an equal; and then a discriminatory war against the East-European and Russian absolute enemies, where all rules of combat and morality were systematically violated and the enemy was considered inhuman.[18] As always, Schmitt neglects to deal with the plight of the European Jewry, against whom Nazi-Germany fought an all-out discriminatory war.

Schmitt failed to ever really engage with the concept of the "total enemy," though the ideological radicalization in the absolute enemy directs our attention to the limitlessness of such an enmity. In the post-war years, however, Schmitt devoted his attention on enmities to the partisan or political struggle enmity forms, while failing to really explore what it means when ideological radicalization merges with state machinery. Raymond Aron, in *Clausewitz—Philosopher of War*, includes a chapter on the partisan, inspired by Schmitt. He criticizes Schmitt, however, not least for the concept of the absolute enemy, which Aron wants to differentiate further between, firstly, a *biologically absolute enmity*: "Ludendorff-Hitler," that is, an enmity based on a biological or racist philosophy: "I would call this 'absolute hostility' as it alone deserves the term 'absolute', since it ends logically in massacre and genocide"[19] and, secondly, an *ideologically absolute enmity*: "Mao-Lenin-Stalin" and in a letter to Schmitt on October 1, 1963, he also mentioned "politically absolute enmity (Carthago for Cato)."[20] Aron

18. Schmitt, *Glossarium*, 117.

19. Aron, *Clausewitz*, 368.

20. Müller, *A Dangerous Mind*, 100.

is, of course, aware that Mao and Stalin murdered more people than Hitler, but that was no logical or necessary consequence of the ideological enmity.

> Hostility based on the class struggle has taken on no less extreme or monstrous forms than that based on the incompatibility of races. But if we wish to 'save the concepts' there is a difference between a philosophy whose logic is monstrous and one which can be given a monstrous interpretation.[21]

In his book, *Democracy and Totalitarianism*, Aron differentiates between the "aim of the Nazi Party," which was "to remake the racial map of Europe and to eliminate certain peoples," and the "aim of Soviet terror . . . to create a society which conforms completely to an ideal, while in the Nazi case, the aim was pure and simple extermination."[22] With Aron, there is not only a differentiation of the totalitarian state enemy but also—like Schmitt but applied to the totalitarian state—a differentiation in stages of enmification or, as he terms it, "three kinds of terror,"[23] which seem to follow Hannah Arendt's differentiation, elaborated below. In concluding this section, it is noted that Aron, while inspired by Schmitt, saw a clear and evident failure on Schmitt's part to apply his enemy theory to the totalitarian state. Once a real totalitarian state came into being in Germany—a qualitatively total state as Schmitt would call it—he suspended his reflections on the enemy, only to return to it in the partisan setting.

In order to understand the peculiarities of the total enemy, it is necessary to depart from the premier theorist of the enemy and take from him only the reflection on the decisive difference between an interstate, codified and hedged 'conventional enmity' and then various forms of unhinged, uncontained enmities, of which Schmitt failed to grasp the most important one. What Schmitt failed to understand was that the state too could be carrier of a completely limitless enmity. To him, it was always state-subversive forces, of which the British Empire was one, that carried such a universalist enmity, never the territorial state. Unlike Schmitt—but with decisive common points of departure[24]—Hannah Arendt made the total enemy a key concept in her explorations of both war and post-war ideological and geopolitical constellations.

---

21. Aron, *Clausewitz*, 369.

22. Aron, *Democracy and Totalitarianism*, 203.

23. Ibid., 187.

24. Bates, "Enemies and Friends"; Sluga, "The pluralism of the political."

Hannah Arendt and the abyss

In a conversation in 1964 with Günter Grass, Hannah Arendt stated what this author takes to be the all-important point of departure in her thoughts on enmity: "Before [the extermination of the Jews] we said: Well, one has enemies. That is entirely natural. Why shouldn't a people have enemies? But this was different. It was really as if an abyss had opened."[25] This indicates a difference between a legitimate, and perhaps containable, enmity and then another much more sinister form which opens the abyss of mass extermination. In her trilogy, *Origins of Totalitarianism*, can be found the fragments of a theory of enmity structured around a distinction between a statist and hedged enmity, the "real enmity," and its more problematic successors in a post nation state reality characterized by the "totalitarian enmity" and the "stateless enmity." These last two are the kinds of enmity that the following will focus on.

The common denominator for the stateless and the totalitarian enmity is what Arendt calls "objective enmity": people being someone's enemies solely because of a being rather than an action, they have made or a threat they constitute. In a proper sense, man's guilt—and thereby the role as enemy—is, according to Arendt, directly derived from its voluntary actions, not its being.[26] Thus, Arendt does not reject enmity as a reality but, rather, insists upon its derivation from actions not from a quality in the enemy. The opposite of the objective enemy is the "real enemy," who correctly or incorrectly is held responsible for a concrete action or as a concrete threat and where the paramount issue is a concrete, detached threat assessment rather than blind hatred. Hatred, Arendt writes, wasn't unknown in the period before the Second World War but now it:

> began to play a central role in public affairs everywhere . . . Nothing perhaps illustrates the general disintegration of political life better than this vague, pervasive hatred of everybody and everything, without a focus for its passionate attention, with nobody to make responsible for the state of affairs—neither the government nor the bourgeoisie nor an outside power. It consequently turned in all directions, haphazardly and unpredictably, incapable of assuming an air of healthy indifference toward anything under the sun.[27]

25. Arendt, "What remains?," 13–14.

26. Arendt, *On Revolution*, 100.

27. Arendt, *Origins of Totalitarianism, vol. II: Imperialism*, 342.

The real enmity and precisely directed hatred are superseded by the generalized enmity and what Arendt above calls a "pervasive hatred of everybody
and everything." The constraints of the real enmity reside in its making
concrete persons or groups responsible for specific actions. Arendt seems
to indicate that real enmity is the paramount form of enmity of the modern nation state with its judicial understanding of the relationship between
state and citizen. The crime and the criminal are the governing language of
the real enmity.

This form of contained enmity is now superseded by a general hatred for everybody and everything just because they happen to be there. A
prominent example is obviously anti-Semitism, where Arendt discerns a
transformation from the crime of Judaism into a vice of Jewishness: "Jews
had been able to escape from Judaism into conversion; from Jewishness
there was no escape. A crime, moreover, is met with punishment; a vice
can only be exterminated."[28] The alleged crime of the Jew, a concrete transgression, is transformed into an abominable and inherent vice: an abstract
being which can only be eradicated through the eradication of the bearers
of the vice.

The real enmity is not spelled out in Arendt's work but has the form
and function as the counter-concept to the post nation state enmities. She
remarks, for instance, that a:

> fundamental difference between modern dictatorships and all
> other tyrannies of the past is that terror is no longer used as a
> means to exterminate and frighten opponents, but as an instru-
> ment to rule masses of people who are perfectly obedient. Terror
> as we know it today strikes without any preliminary provoca-
> tion, its victims are innocent even from the point of view of the
> persecutor.[29]

Totalitarianism, imperialism and statelessness become, for Arendt, the
symbols of the end of the nation state. The important thing is that. with the
end of the nation state, we also witness the decline of the real enmity based
on the perception of real provocations and concrete guilt and the manifestation of forms of enmity that dissolve any relation between action and
hate, guilt and enmity, obedience and protection. The enemy is no longer
he or she that threatens one's existence, but anybody.

28. Arendt, *Origins of Totalitarianism, vol. I: Antisemitism,* 115.
29. Ibid., 14–15.

Totalitarian states do not have enemies in the sense of opponents but only in the sense of enemies till death; that is, totalitarian states do not acknowledge the existence of legitimate others and they have a singular way to deal with enemies, hatred and extermination.

Arendt, like Aron, differentiates between different kinds of terror. The 'tyrannical terror' ends when it has paralyzed or abolished all public life and reduced everyone to lonely individuals without any public interest; 'revolutionary terror' ends when all opposition has been eliminated or the revolution has lost its energy. It is terror "directed toward an end and [which] find an end."[30] However, 'totalitarian terror' is the kind of terror that starts when all real enemies have fled or been killed: when the terror turns on those who are in all senses of the term innocent. Totalitarian terror starts where authoritarian or tyrannical forms of violence stop. Totalitarian terror "turns not only against its enemies but against its friends and supporters as well."[31] In the last chapter of *Totalitarianism*, entitled 'Ideology and Terror: A Novel Form of Government', Arendt characterizes totalitarianism as movement and totalitarian terror as the instrument of that movement:

> Terror is the realization of the law of movement; its chief aim is to make it possible for the force of nature or of history to race freely through mankind, unhindered by any spontaneous human action. As such, terror seeks to 'stabilize' men in order to liberate the forces of nature or history. It is this movement which singles out the foes of mankind against whom terror is let loose, and no free action of either opposition or sympathy can be permitted to interfere with the elimination of the 'objective enemy' of History or Nature, or of the class or the race. Guilt and innocence become senseless notions; 'guilty' is he who stands in the way of the natural or historical process which has passed judgment over 'inferior races', over individuals 'unfit to live', over 'dying classes and decadent peoples'. Terror executes these judgments, and before its court, all concerned are subjectively innocent: the murdered because they did nothing against the system, and the murderers because they do not really murder but execute a death sentence pronounced by some higher tribunal.[32]

Totalitarian terror is used to describe a kind of terror leaving absolutely no freedom or autonomy untouched. It is despotic power in a technological

30. Arendt, "Mankind and Terror," 298.

31. Arendt, *Origins of Totalitarianism, vol. II: Imperialism*, 55.

32. Arendt, *Origins of Totalitarianism, vol. III: Totalitarianism*, 599.

age, making what Montesquieu fantasized about the oriental despotism look and feel like reality. The concept of totalitarian terror draws upon the pre-modern conceptual connection to despotism in emphasizing brutal and not least arbitrary power over individuals but also and significantly the French reign of terror in the emphasis on terror not as an aberration but as a system of rule.

Totalitarianism differs from dictatorships and tyrannies by the grand schemes of methodical mass killing done as a routine part of regime policy: not because the exterminated constitutes an actual threat or opposition, and not because they stand in the way of anything or possesses something the regime wants. It just wants them dead. George Kateb summarizes an essential element in Arendt's definition of totalitarianism when he writes that totalitarian rulers are to be understood "in their essence as mass killers of objectively unthreatening populations in an age where mass killing is easily and antiseptically done."[33]

Totalitarian terror is characterized by a complete indistinction between friends and enemies; it's a distinction which makes no sense for the ideal typical totalitarian, or, rather, comes to be meaningless as the totalitarian movement unfolds:

> [T]otalitarianism defined its enemies ideologically before it seized power, so that categories of the 'suspects' were not established through police information. Thus the Jews in Nazi Germany or the descendants of the former ruling classes in Soviet Russia were not really suspected of any hostile action; they had been declared 'objective' enemies of the regime in accordance with its ideology. The chief difference between the despotic and the totalitarian secret police lies in the difference between the "suspect" and the 'objective enemy'. The latter is defined by the policy of the government and not by his own desire to overthrow it. He is never an individual whose dangerous thoughts must be provoked or whose past justifies suspicion, but a 'carrier of tendencies' like the carrier of a disease . . . The introduction of the notion of 'objective enemy' is much more decisive for the functioning of totalitarian regimes than the ideological definition of the respective categories. If it were only a matter of hating Jews or bourgeois, the totalitarian regime could, after the commission of one gigantic crime, return, as it were, to the rules of normal life and government. As we know, the opposite is the case. The category of objective enemies outlives

33. Kateb, *Hannah Arendt*, 77.

the first ideologically determined foes of the movement; new objective enemies are discovered.[34]

In this last and complete totalitarian stage (which for Arendt presupposes world domination), even the concept of objective enemy is abandoned in favor of a complete arbitrariness in the selection which finally and completely implodes the relation between guilt and enmity. The "all is possible" creed of totalitarianism has its parallel in the claim that any crime is possible or, rather, imaginable and must therefore be punished, even before it is committed or contemplated. The criminal and the law-abiding become indistinct, or, rather again, the distinction itself becomes meaningless. As Primo Levi said upon arriving in Auschwitz: "Here there is no why."[35]

This indistinction and systematized randomness abolishes freedom more effectively than any tyranny could ever do, because at least the notion of being guilty of something in order to be persecuted installed some minimal sense of predictability. In a tyranny, at least one could become guilty, do something to declare oneself or be declared an enemy of the state. The suspected offense of the constitutional state is replaced by the 'possible crime' of the totalitarian state and the "concept of enmity is replaced by that of conspiracy, and this produces a mentality in which reality—real enmity or real friendship—is no longer experienced and understood in its own terms but is automatically assumed to signify something else."[36] In *Modernity and the Holocaust*, Zygmunt Bauman summarizes the totalitarian logic grounded in the belief that "Man *is* before he *acts*; nothing he does may change what he is. This is, roughly, the philosophical essence of racism"[37] and, as seen in the quote from the Cheka at the beginning of this article, this was also the Soviet logic, merely pushing the fault from the bodily to the social genealogy of the individual.

Arendt also draws our attention to the different categories of prisoners in the concentration camps, where "out of racial considerations, Scandinavian nationals during the war were quite differently treated by the Germans than the members of other peoples, although the former were outspoken [real] enemies of the Nazis."[38] This clearly indicates that actually expressed and acted upon enmity or threat was secondary in the Nazi system of enmi-

---

34. Arendt, *Origins of Totalitarianism, vol. III: Totalitarianism*, 548.

35. Semelin, *Purify and Destroy*, 2.

36. Arendt, *Origins of Totalitarianism, vol. III: Totalitarianism*, 551.

37. Bauman, *Modernity and Holocaust*, 60.

38. Arendt, *Origins of Totalitarianism, vol. III: Totalitarianism*, 571.

ty, just as there are important differences between three groups of prisoners whose specific enemy characteristics will be important in the next section: the criminals who "at least know why they are in a concentration camp and therefore have kept a remnant of their judicial person"; the political prisoners for which "this is only subjectively true; their actions, insofar as they were actions and not mere opinions or someone else's vague suspicions, or accidental membership in a politically disapproved group, are as a rule not covered by the normal legal system of the country and not juridically defined"; and, finally, the largest group of people "who had done nothing whatsoever that, either in their own consciousness or the consciousness of their tormenters had any rational connection with their arrest"[39] and who before their physical extermination have been obliterated as juridical persons.

Arendt knew, because of totalitarianism, statelessness on her own body.[40] Further, the parallel between the stateless and the totalitarian enemy becomes evident when she in an article from January 1943, *We Refugees*, writes: "A refugee used to be a person driven to seek refuge because of some act committed or some political opinion held. Well, it is true we have had to seek refuge; but we committed no acts and most of us never dreamt of having any radical political opinion."[41] Perhaps it is more correct to call the stateless a "non-enemy" and thereby reflect on the paradox that it can be worse not being someone's (real) enemy than being nobody's enemy. They are in the juridical sense non-persons because no state takes them seriously as either a responsibility or as a threat:

> [T]he first glaring fact was that these people, though persecuted under some political pretext, were no longer, as the persecuted had been throughout history, a liability and an image of shame for the persecutors; that they were not considered and hardly pretended to be active enemies . . . but that they were and appeared to be nothing but human beings whose very innocence—from every point of view, and especially that of the persecuting government— was their greatest misfortune. Innocence, in the sense of complete lack of responsibility, was the mark of their rightlessness as it was the seal of their loss of political status.[42]

39. Arendt, *Origins of Totalitarianism, vol. III: Totalitarianism*, 578–79.

40. Bernstein, "Hannah Arendt on the Stateless."

41. Arendt, "We Refugees," 55.

42. Arendt, *Origins of Totalitarianism, vol. II: Imperialism*, 374.

Arendt also mentions the importance of the Nazis creating "a condition of complete rightlessness . . . before the right to live was challenged."[43] More important still is what was earlier referred to as the privilege of enmity that the stateless—in addition to a home and government protection—has been robbed of, meaning the minimum protection that comes from being someone's enemy and thereby having a relationship with the enemy other—often even a judicially regulated relationship. No one cares about the fate of the stateless; no one even bothers to declare an enmity: "It seems that a man who is nothing but a man has lost the very qualities which make it possible for other people to treat him as a fellow-man."[44] It is the "loss of a polity [which] expels him from humanity"[45] and makes him or her superfluous, which is the exact relation that totalitarianism has to man: totalitarianism is production of human waste.

Unlike Schmitt, Arendt's view of the modern nation state is ambivalent, sharing with him, on the one side, an understanding of the state as a structure with a demarcated geography constituted by "localized, limited and therefore predictable goals of national interests"; institutionalized in "constitutional restraint"; and "based upon the rule of law as against the rule of arbitrary administration and despotism."[46] Europe's national statesmen "played the game of power politics for the sake of the nation but whose aims were clearly defined and clearly limited."[47] This, despite its excesses and crimes of its own, did limit the more sinister effects and goals of politics. On the other hand, the actual state history is characterized by a linkage between state and nation which transformed the state "from an instrument of law into an instrument of the nation."[48] State history degenerates into the nation conquering the state, in effect dismantling the law's protection of the individual. The transformation from a law-ruled to a culture-ruled state, which is also observable at present, results in Arendt's view in the state beginning to relate to its citizens not by their actions and active choices—and thereby the expression of their individuality and political capacity—but by their abstract or collective being. And to Arendt that is no progress.

43. Ibid., 375.
44. Ibid., 381.
45. Ibid., 377.
46. Ibid., 160–61, 351.
47. Arendt, "Approaches," 108.
48. Arendt, *Origins of Totalitarianism, vol. II: Imperialism*, 296.

Michel Foucault's vital massacres

In the end, Arendt fails to explain the destructive drive of totalitarianism. For her, as for Levi, there is no why: in the end, there is no explanation. It seems the limit of understanding, for Arendt, is grounded in her conception of the modern state as a guardian of life and that the totalitarian state inverts this into a destroyer of life. Committed to a statist understanding, Arendt can ultimately only look at the killing machines with horror. However, as Lifton writes in *The Nazi Doctors*: "At the heart of the Nazi enterprise, then, is the destruction of the boundary between healing and killing," or rather, killing as healing: "*killing as a therapeutic imperative.*"[49] This is the bio-political interpretation which Arendt may have sensed but didn't pursue.

Michel Foucault (and Giorgio Agamben, whose work is inspired by Schmitt, Arendt and Foucault) offers an explanation for the black totalitarianisms, which seems inspired by Arendt (though without any references) while also transcending her analysis by offering a bio-political reading of the same transformation of enmity as Arendt observes. Just as enmity changes, Foucault observes a profound transformation in the concept of war. Ceasing to be primarily outward and contained, war becomes inward and permanent. The line between friends and enemies are doubled inside the territory and is drawn with biological rather than political criteria. It becomes a war not against an armed threat but a pollutant, a degeneracy, an invisible threat coming not from any open enemies but from hidden carriers. Illness rather than opposition becomes the problem; illness equals social disorder, fluid decomposition of order.[50]

This is not the place to rehearse the concept of bio-politics but we can say that it concerns the optimization of life and life processes. It is a politics having life as its goal, object and language and that implodes the differentiation made by Arendt between democratic and totalitarian states. Both have life and its manipulation as their object. Bio-politics is not, as a sovereign power condemning or pardoning any particular person, occupied with the individual but with the population. It wants to intervene in aggregates and it constitutes biological questions of birth, death, age, health, abilities as political problems. Sovereign power is an individualizing power. Bio-politics is a race or species power. The problem is no longer momentary epidemics but statistical occurrences and general trends. Politics is to intervene

49. Lifton, *The Nazi Doctors*, 14, 15.
50. Sontag, *Illness as Metaphor*, chapter 9.

in the background conditions of life at population level, trying to regulate the patterns of life. Bio-politics governs in the service of life and that also means differentiating within life itself between healthy/unhealthy, young/ old, productive/unproductive, culminating in the Nazi concept of "life unworthy to life" [Lebensunwerten Lebens].[51] Bio-politics differentiates between life to be furthered and increased and life to be hindered, reduced, and, ultimately killed.

In the bio-political enmity, the enemy is named in biological and psychological terms and the enemy is found within the social body. The line between an inside—the friends—and an outside—the enemies—is no longer meaningful. The enemy lives among us and the bio-political state takes it upon itself to single out those who threaten the health of the community. This concept of enmity is also highly discriminatory. It establishes a hierarchy of worthy life and starts to talk about "life unworthy of being lived" and its annihilation,[52] most dramatically and tragically executed in the Nazi concentration and euthanasia program but for both Foucault and Agamben a constitutive element in modernity.

This is where health campaigns and extermination programs connect; a connection one shouldn't exaggerate but also not overlook. The Nazis were the first to implement an anti-smoking campaign and we should see this not as the dark secret behind the present health craze but as the range of bio-policies. When, as quoted above, Lifton spoke of "the destruction of the boundary between healing and killing" or the perversion of the Hippocratic Oath into a commitment to killing, we can explore it as the displacement of the oath from the individual body to the national body, from the individual life to the life of the nation. This is what bio-politics does. It views life through a statist, economist, nationalist or racist perspective and it measures its worthiness according to collective standards. The Nazi "invention" or radicalization of bio-politics is to declare war on the unworthy life. Rudolf Hess is supposed to have said that Nazism is applied biology and there is the truth in it that modern racism is a biologization of politics—a biologistic way of defining what used to be the inter-state war of survival but which now becomes the internal war of race survival defending against "the death of the people" [Volkstod].[53] The bio-political war declares war on one's own population:

51. Agamben, *Homo Sacer*, 136–43; Lifton, *The Nazi Doctors*, 46.
52. Agamben, *Homo Sacer*, 136.
53. Savage, "Disease Incarnate."

> [T]he enemies who have to be done away with are not adversaries in the political sense of the term; they are threats, either external or internal, to the population and for the population. In the biopower system, in other words, killing or the imperative to kill is acceptable only if it results not in a victory over political adversaries, but in the elimination of the biological threat to and the improvement of the species or race.[54]

The enemy becomes the abnormal threatening the health of the community. What is to be defended are no longer the outer borders but also and more importantly the reproduction of healthy genes, of optimized life. It is "a racism that society will direct against itself, against its own elements and its own products. This is the internal racism of permanent purification."[55] The enemy is reduced to an obstacle to life's free flow. Life and killing are no longer opposites but preconditions:

> The fact that the other dies does not mean simply that I live in the sense that his death guarantees my safety; the death of the other, the death of the bad race, of the inferior race (or the degenerate, or the abnormal) is something that will make life in general healthier: healthier and purer.[56]

The killing is no longer reduced to war, that is to an exceptional situation of immediate peril, but becomes routine. The heroic battles, looking the enemy in the eye and shooting, are replaced by micro-strategies minimizing the lethality of some while increasing that of others. Killing becomes normal politics, administration. The totalitarian concept of war and enmity implodes the distinction between exception and normalcy, applying the categories and instruments of the exception on everyday life. Totalitarian bio-politics is a generalized state of exception viewing its own population as the object to be defended against itself. It is a shift from citizen to carrier. Spectacular but singular deaths are replaced with statistical death; the sovereign manifestation of power in ritualized executions demonstrating omnipotence is replaced by the operations of the secret police, cattle wagons transporting people away, and death camps far away from public eye. The goal of a bio-political war is not to reach a modus vivendi with the enemy but to eliminate him. This is a total war:

54. Foucault, *Society Must Be Defended*, 256.
55. Ibid., 62.
56. Ibid., 255.

> [T]he enemies who have to be done away with are *not adversaries in the political sense of the term; they are threats,* either external or internal, to the population and for the population. In the biopower system, in other words, killing or the imperative to kill is acceptable only if it results *not in a victory over political adversaries, but in the elimination of the biological threat* to and the improvement of the species or race.[57]

The totalitarian extermination is a system of what Foucault calls vital massacres: vital because they destroy life to enhance life.[58]

There can be no mutuality in the totalitarian enmity. It is a one-sided declaration of war within the social body itself. What the bio-political enmity makes clear is the normalization of the exceptional, as the bio-political state declares war on parts of its own population, not only in form of extermination but also quarantining of the sick, surveillance, exclusions, imprisonments, institutionalization of the abnormal etc. The heroic battles are replaced by micro-technologies that maximize the mortality of some groups and minimize it for others. Instead of individual killings, we get what Ernst Fraenkel with a very precise expression called "civil death"[59] or what Foucault called "statistical death." The sovereign does not manifest himself in splendid displays of power or public executions but in the actions of the secret police, disappearances and extermination camps. The bio-political state emerges where racism and statism meets. Echoing Arendt's remark to Grass about a break in the forms of enmity, Foucault says:

> It is no longer: 'We have to defend ourselves against society', but 'We have to defend society against all the biological threats posed by the other, the subrace, the counterrace that we are, despite ourselves, bringing into existence' ... we see the appearance of a State racism: a racism that society will direct against itself, against its own elements and its own products. This is the internal racism of permanent purification.[60]

The generalization of bio-political technologies marks the breaking point of the difference between norm and exception. In the state of exception, the state can stand in relation of war with its own citizens, the difference between inside (order) and outside (chaos), which informs the norm/

57. Ibid., 256, italics added.
58. Foucault, *The Will to Knowledge*, 137.
59. Fraenkel, *The Dual State*, 95.
60. Foucault, *Society Must Be Defended*, 61–62.

exception, law/lawless, friend/enemy of the national/international divide is doubled within the nation state itself. The borderland is reinstated as the exception. Then, the state becomes, in the words of Agamben, "a killing machine."[61] The breakdown of the differentiations is where the state of exception and bio-politics meet, reaching its ultimate point in Auschwitz where "people did not die; rather, corpses were produced"[62]—meaning this was, in the eyes of the killers, not human life but just inferior biological material to dispose of.

In the bio-political enmity, we can see how arbitrary the dividing line between friend and enemy is. The enemy is not given as enemy, as the many discussions in Nazi circles about who was and who wasn't a Jew testify to. Bio-political enmity is another sign of the difficulties encountered by the state in limiting or containing the enemy category. The bio-political enemy can be everyone—one's blood, heritage, disease or whatever is not necessarily identifiable. Enmity is generalized. The bio-political enmity is perhaps the clearest example of the blurring of differentiations, and it's also where the exception becomes truly permanent. Instead of a war contained in time we get a process of permanent purification, turning ever inwards until self-annihilation; a point on which Foucault and Arendt concur: the logical end point of totalitarianism is suicide.

Total enmity

The German sociologist Wolfgang Sofsky observes a crucial point about the enemy logic behind the concentration camps. The purpose of the social persecution is, as Arendt would concur,

> expulsion and annihilation. Its victims are not to be conquered and forced to obey, but to be removed from society altogether. The targets of terrorist persecution are not so much enemies as strangers and outsiders. These victims may often be described as enemies: enemies of the state, of society, of the people. But this is a wholly misleading redefinition. Enmity is mutual; each side regards the other as its adversary. The persecuted are seen as enemies only by their persecutors.[63]

61. Agamben, *State of Exception*, 86; see also *Means without End*, part 1.
62. Agamben, *Remnants of Auschwitz*, 72.
63. Sofsky, *Violence*, 24-25.

It is not only the sheer enormity of the killings which confounds us. It is also the near complete disconnect between danger and enmity that the totalitarian enemy exhibits. This disconnect turns around everything we think we know about enmification processes; the enemy traditionally being thought as the one out to get us.

What the thinkers above may teach us is that enmity may become so unattached to anything concrete that it can turn all the way around and culminate in a self-enmification. What Carl Schmitt has to offer the analysis of the totalitarian enemy is the logic of enemy escalation: the dichotomy between a hedged, goal-oriented enmity and a globalist "total enmity." What he fails to see is that the real carrier of the "total enmity" is not stateless groups, revolutionary guerillas, nor liberal internationalist powers like Britain or the US; rather, it is states engaging themselves in intensive state-building efforts, sort of halved modernization processes, where only the technical domination aspects and none of the emancipator aspects are forcibly pushed through.

What Hannah Arendt teaches us is exactly the inner logic of this "modernization" process—the functional logic of totalitarian systems—but, ultimately, fails to explain the "why." It has been argued here that we need to turn to a bio-political reading inspired by Michel Foucault. Unlike Schmitt, and to some degree Arendt, he has no strong theory on enemy forms but he has a very clear grasp of how the totalitarian enmity grew out of state logics developed in the centuries before: the telos behind the killings. It is first through Foucault that we get to see what the totalitarian planners were seeing; how and what made sense to them; how it came to be that one could kill on an industrial scale while singing the praises of the vital life. Through this, going from the logic of enmity as such in Schmitt, through the historical reading of state-building in Arendt and to the configurations of radicalized conceptions of life, we learn a lesson: what appears to us as utter destruction was perversely seen by the perpetrators as production.

III

*Private Contemporary Histories
of the Total Enemy*

5

Our Terror, Your Terror: Osama bin Laden on War, Terror, and Enmity

EVERY POWER CLAIMS SOCIAL peace. Every opponent claims social war. And both parties claim being attacked. This is the reality of political struggle. George W. Bush claims the war started on September 11th 2001, whereas Osama bin Laden claims it has been going on for decades. The rebel strategy is to insist on "politics as war" in order to disrupt the legitimizing narrative of the ruling power.

Bush—even despite his one time mention of the war as a "crusade"[1]— repeatedly denied this as a war between religions or civilizations: "There is a great divide in our time—not between religions or cultures, but between civilization and barbarism"[2] and the *National Security Strategy of the United States of America* stated in September 2002: "The war on terrorism is not a clash of civilizations."[3] We may criticize Bush's distinction between civilization and barbarism; however, it is much more important here to note how he rhetorically tries to contain the conflict by insisting that this is not a war of the West versus Muslim countries or Christianity against Islam. Even while talking in war-terms, he, as the representative of existing power, needs to claim a basic social peace only momentarily interrupted.

Osama bin Laden, on the other hand, tries to describe it in more bellicose terms. On October 21, 2001 he said:

1. Bush, "Remarks by the President Upon Arrival."
2. Bush, "President: We're Fighting to Win."
3. US Government, *National Security Strategy of the United States of America*, 31.

> [T]he battle isn't between al Qaeda organization and the global
> Crusaders. Rather, the battle is between Muslims—the people of
> Islam—and the global Crusaders . . . So the world today is split
> in two parts, as Bush said: either you are with us, or you are with
> terrorism. Either you are with the Crusade or you are with Islam .
> . . This [Clash of Civilizations] is a very clear matter.[4]

The conflict is not between two local entities but two universal forces. It is not Al Qaeda fighting but Islam. The US administration keeps insisting upon their benign intentions: "As we strike military targets, we'll also drop food, medicine and supplies to the starving and suffering men and women and children of Afghanistan"[5] whereas Osama bin Laden says: "Do not expect anything from us but jihad, resistance and revenge."[6] Bush says: "We're under attack because we love freedom . . . They hate and we love"[7] whereas bin Laden describes The US as "the butcher of freedom in the world."[8]

In this context, the important thing is not who is right or wrong but the different attempts at describing self and other. Bush describes Al Qaeda as "evil, the very worst of human nature."[9] They are "the enemies of freedom" and "the heirs of all the murderous ideologies of the 20th century"[10] and "a bunch of killers who hate America."[11] Osama bin Laden, on his part, describes his organization as "the victims of murder and massacres . . . defending ourselves against the United States . . . to protect our land and people"[12] and "Al-Qa'idah was set up to wage a jihad against infidelity, particularly to counter the onslaught of the infidel countries against the Islamic states."[13]

Legitimating an armed struggle is to insist that there already is an undeclared war going on and that one is only defending oneself and one's community against oppression. This is not, as the enemy insists, a condition

4. Bin Laden, "Terror for Terror," 108, 121–22, 124.
5. Bush, "Presidential Address to the Nation."
6. Bin Laden, "To the Americans," 164.
7. Bush, "President Bush Calls on Congress."
8. Bin Laden, "Bin-bin Laden tape."
9. Bush, "Statement by the President in His Address to the Nation."
10. Bush, "Address to a Joint Session of Congress and the American People."
11. Bush, "President Bush Calls on Congress to Act on Nation's Priorities."
12. Bin Laden, "The Example of Vietnam," 141.
13. Bin Laden, "Usama bin Laden Says Al-Qa'idah Group."

of peace, but one of war. This article investigates the 'Western side' to al Qaeda, meaning its intervention into the legitimating discourses of political violence. One of the characteristics of the 'new terror' is supposed to be its nihilistic, non-political, non-discursive nature. Yet, al Qaeda may be one of the most talkative terrorist organizations in history. This is most certainly an organization eager to both terrorize and legitimize.

Employing translated texts of Osama bin Laden, mainly from the period 1994-2004, often of uncertain origin and authenticity, this text applies distinctively Western concepts unto non-Western—even anti-Western— texts. Furthermore, while what is offered here is an analysis solely of the texts of Osama bin Laden, the author recognizes that there exist numerous texts of other senior al Qaeda members and training manuals.[14] Presenting neither a novel nor controversial reading of Osama bin Laden, it is, nevertheless, hoped that this text will show how al Qaeda and affiliated organizations actively and offensively engage with Western states and publics, adapting tactics, organization and language to Western traditions and regime forms.

When planes hit in New York and Washington; when bombs go off in London and Madrid; when terror plots are foiled in France, Italy, Denmark, Germany etc., we as Europeans and Westerners naturally assume that it's all about us. We ask: 'Why do they hate *us*?'—assuming that they too consider us the centre of the universe. This study may justly be accused of the same Eurocentrism, even going as far as to reduce the investigated texts to a Western rebel tradition. The excuse, in the form of an explanation, is that *we* can actually understand a lot from this approach and that *they* are in fact both inspired by Western traditions in terms of tactics/strategy (reading Mao, Lenin, Guevara, American military manuals and theorists)[15] and very aware of how to address a Western and a westernized Muslim audience. John Gray says: "There can be no doubt that Al-Qaeda makes use of Islamic traditions, but the belief that the world can be remade by violence is a modern Western inheritance."[16]

The present author is in agreement with Paul Wilkinson, "that what appears to be at first sight a purely religious phenomenon is, in fact, in large

14. Brisard, *Zarqawi*; Cruickshank and Ali, "Abu Musab Al Suri."

15. Stout et al., *The Terrorist Perspectives Project*, chapter 5. See also Cozzens, "Approaching al-Qaeda's warfare"; Brooke, "Jihadist Strategic Debates before 9/11."

16. Gray, "Ever the twain."

part about political control"[17] and with Susan Buck-Morss that Islamism "is the politicization of Islam in a postcolonial context, a contemporary discourse of opposition and debate, dealing with issues of social justice, legitimate power, and ethical life in a way that challenges the hegemony of Western political and cultural norms." Buck-Morss further notes the attempt "to silence Islam as a political discourse, by reducing it to a religious practice." Seeing Islamism as thoroughly modern and political, responding innovatively to present-day pressures "hardly places it beyond criticism,"[18] but it does force us to locate Islamism within the developments we find ourselves confronted with, such as globalization, US hegemony, post-national constellation, global capitalism, human rights regimes, pressures on the 'classical' state, and identity politics etc.

This is not, obviously, to deny the religious component.[19] It is, however, an argument about the priority between a political and a religious interpretation.[20] While the present author is also inclined to agree with those seeing al Qaeda and related groups as deeply connected with and dependent upon a critique of secularism,[21] one should perhaps pause a little before reducing it to a purely religious critique because the alleged effects of secularism being criticized are highly political. The language may—as was the case with Sayyid Qutb who spoke of man usurping God and of how "the world has grown away from religion"[22]—be thoroughly religious, but that is understood here to be a religious language in service of political ends, meaning political rule. Qutb's critique was meant to explain a political failure, namely the humiliation of the Arab states when confronting the Jewish state of Israel and the general decline compared with the West. The explanation became one of a religious secularism critique—"Islam is the

17. Wilkinson, *Terrorism versus Democracy*, 34. Another strong, empirically based argument on the political nature of what would seem at first a religious act is Pape, "The Strategic Logic of Suicide Terrorism."

18. Buck-Morss, *Thinking past terror*, 2, 42, 44.

19. On religion, fundamentalism and violence see Rapoport and Alexander, *The Morality of Terrorism*; Rapoport, "Fear and Trembling"; Juergensmeyer, *Terror in the Mind of God*; Weinberg and Pedahzur, *Religious Fundamentalism and Political Extremism*; Pearce, "Religious Sources of Violence"; Rennie and Tite, *Religion, Terror and Violence*.

20. See the highly interesting essays in Beinin and Stork, *Political Islam*

21. On global anti-secularism see Westerlund, *Questioning the Secular State*; Juergensmeyer, *Global Rebellion*.

22. Qutb, *The Sayyid Qutb Reader*, 157.

solution"[23]—but the purpose was to explain something political. Here, the author concurs with Fred Halliday:

> The overall context is certainly international, that is the subordi-
> nation of these societies to the west, and the rhetoric is gloriously
> eclectic, but the form the revolt takes is primarily revolt against
> the local state. Whatever the transnationalism of disclosure, the
> internationalism of symbol and appeal, and a floating cadre of
> mobile *mujahidin*, the factors that lead to the rise of an Islamist
> movement in, say Iran, Algeria, Afghanistan, Pakistan or Pales-
> tine are those located within that society. In particular they are a
> reaction to the character of the secular state against which these
> movements revolt and of the reforms, of an interventionist and
> secular character, which these states have sought to implement. It
> was, in particular, the secular state's intervention in control of law,
> education, family policy, or the very reaction of society against the
> state's domination of the economy and its associated corruption,
> which explains the rise of Islamist movements in these societies.[24]

And, in continuation, should be added the alleged depletion of military or relational strength vis-à-vis the West and Israel. Islamism was not the first explanation or cure of backwardness but it became the dominant one after the 1970's, leading to an internationalization of explanation and cure, which later opened up for al Qaeda's globalization of interpretation and struggle, turning the local state context into just one more front line struggle. The intention here is to look at how Osama bin Laden justifies his violent ac-tions in a language recognizable for a Western audience.[25] In doing this, the text explores how Osama bin Laden phrases war, terror and enmity, before ending by discussing al Qaeda's innovative difference to most other Islamist groups.

Critique: Declaration of war

The question of Why war? is easily answered when looking through bin Laden's writings and interviews: he is defending Muslims against attacks from the West. One can always recognize someone at war by their acute

23. Wright, *The Looming Tower*, 38.

24. Halliday, *The Middle East in International Relations*, 241.

25. Kennedy, "Is One Person's Terrorist"; Wiktorowicz and Kaltner, "Killing in the Name of Islam"; Wiktorowicz, "A Genealogy of Radical Islam"; International Crisis Group, "In their own words."

and present sense of history: no injury or violation is forgotten; nothing is in the past; everything done has contemporary consequences; the enemy has been the same throughout history; and Osama bin Laden repeatedly stresses the historic onslaught on Muslims—although his main concern is the present-day atrocities in Palestine, Chechnya, Bosnia-Herzegovina, Iraq etc. and the alleged occupation or domination of Muslim lands especially on the Arabian Peninsula. One can dispute his real interest in the plight of these peoples and countries but they are, nevertheless, very actively used to convey the message of a massive and ongoing onslaught on Muslims worldwide: under attack for the simple reason that they are Muslims.

If one wants to understand Osama bin Laden and the attraction of his message, one has to grasp this feeling of being under attack: "We are only defending ourselves. This is defensive Jihad. We want to defend our people and our land."[26] The supposed aggressor need not perceive or describe it as such for it to be felt this way. Just like George W. Bush claimed that war was forced upon The US and the world on September 11, 2001, Osama bin Laden stresses that the attacks are coming from the West and have been going on for decades: "We are being violated in Palestine, in Iraq, in Lebanon, in Sudan, in Somalia, in Kashmir, in the Philippines, and throughout the world."[27]

This situation has left no other choice than counter-attack: "We have been violated, so our first duty is to remove this violation."[28] His analysis is "that the situation cannot be rectified . . . unless the root of the problem is tackled. Hence it is essential to hit the main enemy who divided the umma into small and little countries and pushed it, for the last few decades, into a state of confusion."[29] This means directing the fire against the primary target of America. The dividing line seems clear: "Our enemy is the crusader alliance led by America, Britain and Israel. It is a crusader-Jewish alliance,"[30] ultimately leading to a defining dichotomy between the "international crusaders and the Jewish-Zionist alliance headed by America, Britain and Israel. The second party is the Islamic world."[31] However, looking further, a number of differentiations, different forms of enmity and different categories of enemies become apparent:

26. Bin Laden, "Usama bin Laden: Interview with 'Dawn' and 'Ausaf.'"
27. Bin Laden, "Terror for Terror," 112–13.
28. Bin Laden, "Terror for Terror," 126.
29. Bin Laden, "Declaration of Jihad."
30. Bin Laden, "Interview with John Miller, ABC News."
31. Bin Laden, "Interview with al-Jazira."

Internal Enemies: Protection and Purity. An important distinction is made between internal and external enemies. Turning attention first to the internal—that is Muslim—enemies, it shouldn't be forgotten that a significant part of Osama bin Laden's critique is directed against 1) the leaders/regimes of Muslim countries; 2) religious teachers close to the regimes; 3) apathetic and/or westernized Muslims; and that a large number of their victims have been Muslims.

Osama bin Laden reportedly tried to influence the Saudi leadership prior to the first Gulf war, warning them against inviting US troops to defend the country against Saddam Hussein. After the king's decision to let US troops defend the holy sites, bin Laden turned against the Saudi royal family while still lobbying them with letters and petitions, and by rallying religious scholars and so on.[32] He obviously felt harassed (probably rightly so) and left for Sudan: "Why is it then that the regime closed all peaceful routes and pushed the people toward armed actions, which are the only choice left for them to implement righteousness and justice?"[33]

The fault of the Arab regimes is both political and religious: they haven't defended the independence and sovereignty of their countries and they haven't upheld the true faith in their system of rule; they have implemented man-made laws and allowed Western ideas of banking, civil society, democracy etc. to creep in and subvert the religious foundation of political power; the political leadership has sold out politically and religiously, failing to defend Muslim freedom as peoples and as believers.

This leads directly to the critique of the Muslim regimes. In March 1997, he said of Saudi Arabia that "the regime has stopped ruling people according to what God revealed . . . When this main foundation was violated, other corrupt acts followed in every aspect of the country, the economic, the social, the public services and so on."[34] The problem of the current Muslim regimes is that they have strayed from the true course which includes a religious and a political duty. The religious duty is to stay true to the Islamic teachings; Osama bin Laden repeatedly criticizes Muslim regimes for their alleged secularism: "[s]ince the fall of the Islamic Caliphate state, regimes that do not rule according to the Qur'an have arisen. If truth be told, these regimes are fighting against the law of God."[35]

32. Anonymous, *Through Our Enemies' Eyes*, 114.
33. Bin Laden, "Declaration of Jihad."
34. Bin Laden, "From Somalia to Afghanistan," 45.
35. Bin Laden, "Bin Ladin audiotape attacking Muslim scholars."

The second duty is political, or politico-religious: the defense of Muslim territory. Instead, they have allowed it to "become an American colony."[36] This clearly shows the two main political goals of Osama bin Laden: independence and reformation of the Muslim countries. Foreign elements have polluted Islam: US soldiers and Western ideas. The prime task is to restore purity. The geopolitical goal is to restore Muslim dominance of, firstly, the Arabian Peninsula, and, secondly, every other Muslim country. The politico-religious goal is to islamicize the rule. Independence from the outside and Islam on the inside will lead to the third and final, religious goal: a re-moralization of Muslims who have become materialistic, apathetic, individualistic etc.

The accusation against the religious scholars and teachers are obvious. They have sold out the true faith for a seat near the political power. The danger stemming from this is greater than ever before: "[t]he nation has never been as damaged by a catastrophe like the one that damages them today. In the past, there was imperfection, but it was partial. Today, however, the imperfection touches the entire public because of the communications revolution and because the media enter every home."[37] The early texts of Osama bin Laden concentrated quite a lot on the religious and political misinterpretations of the scholars. It seems that since al Qaeda has built up an effective communication system of its own, effectively bypassing the established religious channels of communication, he has stopped spending much time on them. Their "misinterpretation" of the Quran and critique of him becomes a license to interpret the holy texts by a non-scholar. He has gone from trying to solicit their help to ignoring them (though, as we shall touch upon later, al Qaeda has been forced into a renewed "debate" with Islamic scholars criticizing their terrorism).

The final form of internal enemy, and clearly that which troubles Osama bin Laden the most, is the question of why Muslims are not rising in greater numbers: "why do Muslims hold back from helping their religion?"[38] "Afghanistan is [but] a few hours away from the Arabian Peninsula, or from any of the countries of the Islamic world . . . but the Taliban state disappeared, and they did not lift a finger."[39] As for every insurgent or terrorist group, the puzzle of civil non-resistance is a source of bewilderment and

36. Bin Laden, "Osama bin Laden. Interview by Robert Fisk."
37. Bin Laden, "Bin Ladin audiotape attacking Muslim scholars."
38. Bin Laden, "Interview with John Miller, ABC News."
39. Bin Laden, "Bin Ladin audiotape attacking Muslim scholars."

frustration. This enemy can be divided into three forms, each with a still higher degree of enmity: firstly, the common Muslim who doesn't react when his fellow believers are being attacked; secondly, those who participate in what he describes as un-Islamic activities—voting, working for apostate regimes—and who, therefore, in effect, become non-believers; thirdly, there are the actual internal enemies—those who, according to bin Laden, engage in anti-Islamic activities—people in power, soldiers and policemen—as apostates, tyrants, caliphs, and, therefore, fair game.

A distinction can be included between different schools of Islam: most notably between shia and sunni; however, this doesn't seem to concern Osama bin Laden much, perhaps because of the common larger foe. Al Qaeda appears to combine religious fanaticism with extreme pragmatism and strategism. Speaking of Iraq, he said that "there is no harm in such circumstances if the Muslims' interests coincide with those of the [Iraqi Baathist] socialists in fighting the Crusaders, despite our firm conviction that they are infidels."[40] It seems the internal enemy is employed very strategically. The internal enemy is a second order enemy.

External enemies: Crusade and Occupation. The external enemy, on the other hand, is a first order enemy. This enemy also has the accelerating feature of being easily distinguished as outsider. Mark Juergensmeyer follows the main interpretation of Islamist terror and enmity by explaining (or reducing) it to religious motivation:

> Everyone has enemies in the sense of opponents, but to become objects of religious terrorism such enemies must become extraordinary: cosmic foes. When Osama bin Laden spoke of America as embodying the 'forces of evil', he was not just identifying a problem to which he needed to respond, but a mythic monster with which he had to battle—one that ultimately only divine power could subdue. The question is how this happened—how a view of an opponent could cross the line into a deep and enduring hatred for a satanic entity. I call this process satanization.[41]

It is an interpretation, with which the present author is in agreement, of the religious enemy and its result in 'sacred terror.'[42] However, it is argued here that it is necessary to differentiate between two enmities in Osama bin Laden's texts, often intertwined in the actual argument, but which are, however,

40. Bin Laden, "To the People of Iraq," 184.
41. Juergensmeyer, *Terror in the Mind of God*, 182.
42. Rapoport, "Sacred terror."

quite distinct: namely, a *religious enmity* which pits a global and eternal enmity between Christianity and Judaism on one side and Islam on the other, and a *political enmity* which concerns the West's alleged occupation and domination of Muslim lands. The first form of enmity is perpetual; it has no possibility for peace (but for cease-fire, as we'll see later); it is a fight to the death. The religious enmity is total, global and highly asymmetrical. The political enmity, on the other hand, is limited; it contains some form of symmetry; it could give way for co-existence given the cessation of its causes, namely occupation and humiliation.

In the actual texts, there is seldom a clear differentiation between the two but I would argue that it is essential for understanding (and possibly also for containing the conflict) to distinguish between these two forms, which should be thought of as different (and simultaneous) *logics of enmity* rather than as actual discrete forms. One thing blurring the picture is Osama bin Laden's invocation of both logics in his description of the enemy as "the Crusader-Jewish forces of occupation."[43] What should one think of the claim that the peoples of the Arabian Peninsula have "never suffered such a calamity as these Crusader hordes that have spread through it like locusts, consuming and destroying its fertility,"[44] that "the greatest unbelief, the Crusader-American alliance, remains unchallenged, tearing the Islamic world apart and plundering the wealth of Muslims in an unprecedented manner,"[45] or when Osama bin Laden is "calling on the Islamic nation to carry on jihad aimed at liberating holy sites."[46]

They may be given both a political and a religious interpretation and it may be that Western modern-secular concepts obscure the indistinction between (the Western concepts of) religion and politics possibly inherent in Islam. Osama bin Laden stated the indistinction when he termed the conflict "a religious-economic war. They want the believers to desist from worshipping God so that they can enslave them, occupy their countries, and loot their wealth."[47] Similarly, the often used word of "crusade" testifies to a religious conflict whereas the just as often used word of "occupation" hints at a political conflict. Still, the distinction is easily observable in the texts. On the one hand we have the religious enmity:

43. Bin Laden, "The Betrayal of Palestine," 9.
44. Bin Laden, "The World Islamic Front," 59.
45. Bin Laden, "A Muslim Bomb," 89.
46. Bin Laden, "Wrath of God."
47. Bin Laden, "Resist the New Rome," 214.

the neo-Crusader-Jewish campaign led by Bush, the biggest Crusader, under the banner of the cross. This battle can be seen as merely one of the battles of eternal Islam.[48]

This war is fundamentally religious. The people of the East are Muslims. They sympathized with Muslims against the people of the West, who are the crusaders. Those who try to cover this crystal clear fact, which the entire world has admitted, are deceiving the Islamic nation. They are trying to deflect the attention of the Islamic nation from the truth of this conflict. This fact is proven in the book of God Almighty and in the teachings of our messenger, may God's peace and blessings be upon him. Under no circumstances should we forget this enmity between us and the infidels. For the enmity is based on creed.[49]

It has become all too clear that the West in general, with America at its head, carries an unspeakable Crusader hatred for Islam.[50]

How can intelligent people believe that yesterday's enemies on the basis of religion can become today's friends? This can only happen if one of the two parties abandons his religion.[51]

This reasoning clearly states it as a religious conflict about ultimate values and eternal enemies. The enemy is inflated into the abstraction of "the West" and "Christianity," just like other rebel groups speak of "the system" as an all-encompassing entity. However, a different line of enmity logic reveals another set of explanations for the present conflict, another demarcation and, ultimately, another kind of war:

The solution to this crisis is the withdrawal of American troops . . . their military presence is an insult for the Saudi people.[52]

It is not a declaration of war—it's a real description of the situation. This doesn't mean declaring war against the West and Western people—but against the American regime which is against every Muslim.[53]

48. Bin Laden, "To our brothers in Pakistan," 101.
49. Bin Laden, "Osama bin Laden on al-Jazira."
50. Bin Laden, "Nineteen Students," 146.
51. Bin Laden, "Fight On, Champions of Somalia."
52. Bin Laden, "Interview with Robert Fisk."
53. Ibid.

> Why are we fighting and opposing you? The answer is very simple:
> Because you attacked us and continue to attack us . . . You steal our
> wealth and oil at paltry prices because of your international influ-
> ence and military threats. . . . Your forces occupy our countries .
> . . You have starved the Muslims of Iraq . . . You have supported
> the Jews.[54]

The political enmity is concrete; it concerns occupation and domination.
Norman Fairclough writes in *Language and Globalization*: "One may not
see these reasons as justifying terrorism, but they are reasons."[55]

One can speculate about whether The US or Israel/Jews are the main
enemy. A case could be made that Israel/Jews are enemy number one and
The US is "merely" the protector of Israel/Jews or possibly its puppet, which
needs to be overcome before the final and actual battle: "[t]he American
president and his administration are under the influence of the Jewish Zionist lobby in America, who are pushing the American people to do what
Israel cannot do."[56]

Peter Bergen states that Osama bin Laden, upon his return to Saudi
Arabia from Afghanistan, urged people to boycott US products because
of its support of Israel.[57] Still, there has been a remarkable 'lack' of attacks
against Jewish targets, suggesting it may not be the primary target or that
Osama bin Laden reckons Israel will collapse once The US is gone or
weakened.[58] Be that as it may, the enmity towards Israel/Jews is of a more
religious nature than that directed against Americans. It still has a political
dimension, however, which is Israel's damaging influence upon the Arab
world; he repeatedly emphasizes "the Jews' violation of Palestine."[59] However, the religious dimension is more dominant and there seems to be no
option other than the destruction of Israel and the exodus of Jews. It is also
significant that Osama bin Laden does not even attempt a distinction between Israel as a country or state and the Jews as a people, which is why this
external enemy is here referred to as "Israel/Jews." The enmity is often just
stated as a fact needing no further explanation or justification: "The current
Jewish enemy is not an enemy settled in his own original country fighting

54. Bin Laden, "To the Americans,", 162–64.
55. Fairclough, *Language and Globalization*, 151.
56. Bin Laden, "Interview with Jamal Isma'il, al-Jazira."
57. Bergen, *Holy War, Inc*, 77.
58. Anonymous, *Through Our Enemies' Eyes*, 231–33.
59. Bin Laden, "The Invasion of Arabia," 17.

in its defense until he gains a peace agreement, but an attacking enemy and a corrupter of religion and the world."[60] That enmity is eternal. The Jews will be an enemy with or without the state of Israel. This is the most pure expression of a religious enmity: enmity based on being rather than acting.

Combat: Methodology of war

Primarily, al Qaeda is known as a terror organization and Osama bin Laden as a terrorist. This has, however, not sparked many explorations into what bin Laden has to say about terrorism, its justification, purpose or method.[61] A few thoughts are presented here to this effect in an attempt to understand how he can justify horrendous acts and what he thinks they can achieve.

A first and important observation, which he shares with almost all wielders of organized violence in conflicts, is the argument that all of his actions are culpable upon the opponent as the instigator of the conflict. A preliminary conclusion is given by Mark Juergensmeyer, writing that "if the world is perceived as peaceful, violent acts appear as terrorism. If the world is thought to be at war, violent acts may be regarded as legitimate."[62] Actions interpreted in the West as aggressive and unprovoked acts of terrorism, are, for Osama bin Laden, legitimate acts of self-defense in an undeclared and ongoing Western-led war against the Muslim world.

We may not perceive such a war taking place but it is real for bin Laden and his followers. We may explain his justification of defensive terrorism as a case of what Maurice Tugwell calls "guilt transfer"; that is, "a switch of public attention away from embarrassing acts of its originator toward the embarrassing acts of the adversary, so that the former may be forgotten or forgiven while the latter erode the confidence and legitimacy of the other side."[63] That would however fail to give an understanding of his motives. It is asserted here that the proper way to understand this is to take his statements seriously as genuine expressions of feelings of humiliation pushed into the war narrative. The theory of guilt transfer may be

60. Bin Laden, "The Betrayal of Palestine," 9.

61. For studies investigating the "al Qaeda ideology" or the "Islamist ideology" more broadly and taking both the religion and the politics seriously see Scheffler, "Apocalypticism"; Sedgwick, "Al-Qaeda and the Nature of Religious Terrorism"; McAuley, "The ideology of Osama bin Laden"; Andersen, *Innocence Lost*; Steger, *The Rise of the Global Imaginary*, chap. 6; Lia, "Al-Qaida's Appeal."

62. Juergensmeyer, *Terror in the Mind of God*, 9.

63. Tugwell, "Guilt Transfer," 57.

correct in explaining how the justifying argument for committed terrorism is formulated; it does not, however, explain why the terrorism was decided and executed in the first place. For that, it is necessary to go to the source of both the terror and its justification.

The Myth of US Superiority. In the US 1997 *Quadrennial Defense Review*, it was observed that "US dominance in the conventional military arena may encourage adversaries to use . . . asymmetric means to attack our interests and Americans at home"[64] and in the 2006 manual of counterinsurgency: "[b]ecause the United States retains significant advantages in fires and technical surveillance a thinking enemy is unlikely to choose to fight U.S. forces in open battle."[65] This is also what Osama bin Laden observed, when he in 1996 addressed Saudi military forces: "it must be obvious to you that, due to the imbalance of power between our armed forces and the enemy forces, a suitable means of fighting must be adopted, i.e. using fast moving light forces that work under complete secrecy. In other words: to initiate guerrilla warfare."[66]

Attacking The US can only be done asymmetrically—even by a symmetric enemy (this explains Iran's statement in the early 2000's, that they, even as a conventional state and army, have thousands of suicide-warriors awaiting US attack). Terrorism is truly the instrument of the weak and, paradoxically, all opponents the US can be expected to resort to it because The US is actively pursuing a policy of making their armed forces "strong enough to dissuade potential adversaries from pursuing a military build-up in hopes of surpassing, or equalling, the power of the United States."[67] The denial of symmetry leaves only the asymmetrical option of terrorism and guerrilla warfare.

The rationality behind Osama bin Laden's terror campaign is one of strength and weakness. A Taleban fighter, in all likelihood now dead, said about his US counterpart in a statement highly reminiscent of every reactionary political organization in modern political thought: "They love Pepsi-Cola, but we love death."[68] This is the operational doctrine behind al Qaeda's war strategy, that the US can be terrorized into withdrawal or even submission while Muslims, through a cult of death, are undefeatable.

64. Freedman, "The Third World War?," 70.
65. US Army, *Counterinsurgency*, §1.8.
66. Bin Laden, "Declaration of Jihad."
67. US Government, *National Security Strategy*, 30.
68. Buruma and Margalit, *Occidentalism*, 49.

Numerous are the statements about the Muslim fighter's embrace of death: "We love this kind of death for God's cause as much as you like to live. We have nothing to fear for. It is something we wish for."[69] And: "O youth of the nation. Crave death and life will be given to you."[70] Fighting to the death becomes the proof of living: "You fight, so you exist."[71] That is common belief among all reactionary movements and which is well-known from European fascism and Nazism.[72]

This only gains real meaning against an enemy who value life and death differently. Osama bin Laden repeatedly stresses the supposed cowardice of Americans. It's important for him to dispel the "myth" of the US war machine, expose "the low spiritual morale of the American fighters," and stress their "successive defeats in Vietnam, Beirut, Aden, and Somalia."[73] The experience of the war between the Soviet Union and Afghanistan taught him the emptiness of secularism and materialism when faced with belief and spirit: "they [the Afghans and the 'Afghan Arabs'] managed to destroy the myth of the largest military machine ever known to mankind and utterly annihilated the idea of the so-called superpowers. We believe that America is much weaker than Russia, and we have learned from our brothers who fought in the jihad in Somalia of the incredible weakness and cowardice of the American soldier."[74] He keeps returning to the experience of Beirut and Somalia to illustrate his belief that the Americans "are the most cowardly people in battle."[75] It is this belief which makes it plausible for him that terror is an effective weapon. The "force-protection fetishism"[76] of US "post-heroic warfare"[77] contra the "death fetishism" of Islamic "heroic warfare" opens the possibility of bleeding and horrifying the Americans into retreat.

It is very important for Osama bin Laden to make a case for US vulnerability. We can illustrate that with a short discussion of how Osama bin Laden has interpreted the fall of the Twin Towers as evidence of his

69. Bin Laden, "From Somalia to Afghanistan," 56.

70. Bin Laden, "Osama bin Laden on al-Majalla."

71. Bin Laden, "Resist the New Rome," 231.

72. Neocleous, "Long live death!"

73. Bin Laden, "From Somalia to Afghanistan," 54–55. See also Stout et al., *The Terrorist Perspectives Project*, 95–104.

74. Bin Laden, "A Muslim Bomb," 82.

75. Bin Laden, "Among A Band of Knights," 191.

76. Freedman, "The Third World War?," 72.

77. Luttwak, "Towards Post-Heroic Warfare."

approach to the Islamic struggle. September 11 "shifted the battle to the heart of the United States" and "destroyed its most outstanding landmarks, its economic and military landmarks."[78] The Twin Towers are seen as both the actual and symbolic entity of US power. Al Qaeda . . .

> attacked the biggest center of military power in the world, the Pentagon, which contains more than 64,000 workers, a military base which has a big concentration of army and intelligence . . . As for the World Trade Center, the ones who were attacked and who died in it were part of a financial power. It wasn't a children's school! Neither was it a residence. And the general consensus is that most of the people who were in the towers were men that backed the biggest financial force in the world, which spreads mischief throughout the world.[79]

> But I mention that there are also other events that took place, bigger, greater, and more dangerous that the collapse of the towers. It is that this Western civilization, which is backed by America, has lost its values and appeal. The immense materialistic towers, which preach Freedom, Human Rights, and Equality, were destroyed. These values were revealed as a total mockery.[80]

> So they attacked the enemy with their own planes in a brave and beautiful operation, the like of which humanity has never seen before, destroying the idols of America. They struck at the very heart of the Ministry of Defense, and they hit the American economy right at its heart, too. They rubbed America's nose in the dirt, and wiped its arrogance in the mud. As the twin towers of New York collapsed, something even greater and more enormous collapsed with them: the myth of the great America and the myth of democracy.[81]

The "storm of planes" destroyed, according to bin Laden, the myth of US invulnerability and superiority, and "the icons of military and economic power"[82] furthermore, it seems (even after the attack on Afghanistan) to have confirmed his view on US combat readiness: "Don't let their numbers frighten you, for their hearts are empty and they are falling into military and economic disarray, especially after the blessed day in New York, by the

78. Bin Laden, "Terror for terror," 107.

79. Ibid., 119.

80. Ibid., 112.

81. Bin Laden, "Among A Band of Knights," 194.

82. Bin Laden, "Usama bin Laden: Interview with 'Dawn' and 'Ausaf.'"

grace of God."[83] Invulnerability must be exposed. The visible inequality of force must be denied: "I assure you that the Zionist entity reining over the land of Palestine is a very fragile entity, and has many weak points."[84] If it did not, struggle would be useless.

The 9/11 attack, more than any text of Osama bin Laden, convinced many radical(ized) Islamists of the truth of not only his strategy but also his message. It opened, so to speak, a room of possibility and it exposed the front lines: "[o]ne of the most important positive effects of our attacks on New York and Washington was to expose the reality of the struggle between the Crusaders and the Muslims . . . The entire world woke up from its slumber, and the Muslims realized the importance of the doctrine of friendship and enmity in God."[85]

Not only did the attack and its aftermath force a taking of sides. It also revealed a weakness in the heart of the greatest economy and war machine in human history. The attacks revealed for bin Laden and his followers that The US could be attacked on its own soil; that it was possible to bring violence to its shores; that The US could be reached. The attacks revealed that this was not what most other opposition movements had long thought a time of no alternatives and no real struggles. It was, according to bin Laden, a revolutionary time where not only struggle but also victory was possible.

Lawrence Freedman says that unlike conventional armies, terrorists and guerrillas "need time more than space, for it is their ability to endure while mounting regular attacks that enables them to grow while the enemy is drained of patience and credibility."[86] Terrorist groups do not aim to hold land, as an army does; it seeks to dominate time in the form of endurance and patience in struggle. This is the strategy of al Qaeda: to use The US's dependence on space (homeland, embassies, military bases, and tourist resorts) and its own endurance of time; US locality versus Islamist eternity:

> Days and nights will not go by until we take revenge as we did on
> 11 September, God willing, and until your minds are exhausted
> and your lives become miserable and things turn [for the worse]
> which you detest . . . As for us, we do not have anything to lose. The
> swimmer in the sea does not fear rain. You have occupied our land,
> defiled our honour, violated our dignity, shed our blood, ransacked

83. Bin Laden, "Quagmires of the Tigris and Euphrates," 210.

84. Bin Laden, "Message to the Islamic Nation on 60th Anniversary of Israel."

85. Bin Laden, "Among A Band of Knights," 194.

86. Freedman, "The Third World War?," 67.

our money, demolished our houses, rendered us homeless, and
tampered with our security. We will treat you in the same way.[87]

Osama bin Laden is therefore repeatedly stressing both their love of death
and their patience: "Mujahidin, be patient and think of the hereafter, for
this path in life requires sacrifices, maybe with your life. You scare the enemy but they do not scare you."[88] It's not their ability to conquer the enemy,
which can assure them victory, but their ability to endure beyond the military and economic capacity of its enemy.

Good and Bad Terrorism. "Our terrorism against America is a praiseworthy terrorism in defense against the oppressor, in order that America
will stop supporting Israel, who kills our sons. Can you not understand
this? It is very clear."[89] Unlike the main tendency of most actors labelled as
'terrorist', Osama bin Laden has somewhat embraced the concept of terrorism and used it quite offensively. Not only does he return the epithet but
takes it upon himself as a description of fact: terror for terror.

This apparent symmetry is imploded, however, by the distinction
between an offensive and malignant terrorism executed by the Americans
and a defensive and benign terrorism wielded by al Qaeda. We have two
co-existing logics: firstly, the logic that both sides employ terrorism—moral
equalization; terrorism is just an instrument among others, making it is
hypocritical for Westerners to label only al Qaeda terrorists: "If we try to
defend ourselves, they call us 'terrorists', and the slaughter still goes on."[90]
"When they wanted to combat the summit of the hump of Islam, Jihad in
Allah's path, they labelled it 'violence' and 'terrorism'."[91] This logic also ad-
vocates a similarity of suffering; an implicit notion of a common humanity
even: "Who said that our blood isn't blood and that their blood is blood?"[92]
Secondly, there is the logic that distinguishes between offensive and defensive terrorism—moral hierarchization—where al Qaeda is employing
terrorism to stop the greater, offensive terrorism. Terror becomes a tool to
scare and frighten the US into retreat: "just as you bomb, so you shall be
bombed. And there will be more to come."[93]

87. Bin Laden, "Bin-bin Laden tape."
88. Bin Laden, "Depose the Tyrants," 272.
89. Bin Laden, "Nineteen Students," 152.
90. Bin Laden, "Terror for terror," 125.
91. Bin Laden, "Practical Steps to Liberate Palestine."
92. Bin Laden, "Terror for terror," 117.
93. Bin Laden, "To the Allies of America," 175.

The purpose of the first logic is to question the claim to security of the US and Western publics. Osama bin Laden says: "We have been fighting you because we are free men who cannot acquiesce in injustice. . . . Just as you violate our security, so we violate yours. Whoever encroaches upon the security of others and imagines that he will himself remain safe is but a foolish criminal."[94] Further, and more to the point: "How can they hope to be blessed with security while they are dishing out destruction, devastation, and murder on our people in Palestine and Iraq?"[95]

The exposure to or threat of terror is not, bin Laden argues, as the *National Security Strategy of the United States of America* states, "a new condition of life"[96] but a choice: "So the Westerners are free to choose. Europe wants to enter the war—that is their prerogative, but our duty is to fight whoever is in the ranks of the Jews. America and the American people are free; they have entered the trench, and they will get what is coming to them."[97] Terror against Muslims is now, Osama bin Laden says, being met with terror against Westerners:

> God has struck America at its Achilles heel and destroyed its greatest buildings . . . America has been filled with terror from north to south and from east to west . . . What America is tasting today is but a fraction of what we have tasted for decades. For over eighty years our umma has endured this humiliation and contempt. Its sons have been killed, its blood has been shed, its holy sanctuaries have been violated, all in a manner contrary to that revealed by God, without any listening or responding.[98]

> So, as they kill us, without a doubt we have to kill them, until we obtain a balance in terror. This is the first time, in recent years, that the balance of terror has evened out between the Muslims and the Americans; previously, the Americans did to us whatever they pleased, and the victim wasn't even allowed to complain.[99]

He is, then, advocating symmetry of terror, a terror balance, to equalize the pain and suffering, insisting on the equal worth of Muslim lives and insisting that a life lived in security is "a legitimate right, well known to

94. Bin Laden, "The Towers of Lebanon," 238.

95. Bin Laden, "Depose the Tyrants," 270.

96. US Government, *National Security Strategy*, 31.

97. Bin Laden, "Terror for terror," 128.

98. Bin Laden, "The Winds of Faith," 104.

99. Bin Laden, "Terror for terror," 114.

all humans and other creatures,"[100] the violation of which gives a similar legitimate right to resistance and tyrannicide:

> [T]errorism can be commendable and it can be reprehensible. Terrifying an innocent person and terrorizing him is objectionable and unjust, also unjustly terrorizing people is not right. Whereas, terrorizing oppressors and criminals and thieves and robbers is necessary for the safety of the people and the protection of their property. There is no doubt in this. Every state and every civilization and culture has to resort to terrorism under certain circumstances for the purpose of abolishing tyranny and corruption. Every country in the world has its own security system and its own security forces, its own police and its own army. They are all designed to terrorize whoever even contemplates to attack that country or its citizens. The terrorism we practise is of the commendable kind for it is directed at the tyrants and the aggressors and the enemies of Allah.[101]

> So, not all terrorism is restrained or ill-advised. There is terrorism that is ill-advised and there is terrorism that is a good act. So, in their definition of the word, if a criminal or a thief feels that he is terrorized by the police, do we label the police terrorists and say they terrorized the thief? No, the terrorism of the police towards the criminals is a good act, and the terrorism that is being exercised by the criminals against the true believers is wrong and ill-advised. So America and Israel practise ill-advised terrorism, and we practice good terrorism, because it deters those from killing our children in Palestine and other places.[102]

The terrorism of "the police" is well-advised because its purpose is to halt violence, whereas the terrorism of "the criminal" is ill-advised, immoral even, because it perpetuates violence.

The Killing of Civilians: Innocence and Guilt. Throughout bin Laden's texts there are two main approaches to the question of the killing of civilians. The first is that it is against the teachings of Islam; that al Qaeda refrains from targeting civilians (it is the Americans who are killing civilians); and that they in general differentiate between the system and the people and between soldiers/politicians and civilians. This position is unsustainable

---

100. Bin Laden, "Declaration of Jihad."
101. Bin Laden, "Interview with John Miller, ABC News."
102. Bin Laden, "Terror for terror," 120.

because al Qaeda needs to respond to the glaring fact that non-combatants are deliberately targeted.

The second approach explodes the distinction, stating that it is illogical and that (almost) every American or Westerner is a legitimate target. In a 2002 al Qaeda document "regarding the mandates of the heroes and the legality of the operations in New York and Washington," a number of explanations can be found for the killing of innocents:[103]

- All wars have collateral damage

    → the killing of civilians as *unfortunate*

- The necessity of war and the nature of the target makes the distinction between civilians and combatants impossible

    → the killing of civilians as *unintended*

    "It is allowed for Muslims to kill protected ones among unbelievers in the event of an attack against them in which it is not possible to differentiate the protected ones from the combatants or from the strongholds. It is permissible to kill them incidentally and unintentionally."

    "It is allowed for Muslims to kill protected ones among unbelievers in the event of a need to burn the strongholds or fields of the enemy so as to weaken its strength in order to conquer the stronghold or topple the state."

    "It is allowed for Muslims to kill protected ones among unbelievers when they are using heavy weapons that do not distinguish between combatants and protected ones."

    "It is allowed for Muslims to kill protected ones among unbelievers when the enemy is shielded by their women or children."

- Civilians are not innocent because they vote and pay taxes (serve in the military and reserve service as all Israelis do), directly and indirectly supporting the onslaught on innocent Muslims

    → the killing of civilians is *legitimate*

    "It is allowed for Muslims to kill protected ones among unbelievers on the condition that the protected ones have assisted

103. Al Qaeda, "Statement from qaidat al-jihad."

in combat, whether in deed, word, mind, or any other form of assistance."

"It is allowed for Muslims to kill protected ones among unbelievers if the people of a treaty violate their treaty and the leader must kill them in order to teach them a lesson."

- Civilians are in fact innocent but their killing is justified because that is how our innocents are treated

  → the killing of civilians is *justified by their leader's actions*

  "It is allowed for Muslims to kill protected ones as an act of reciprocity. If the unbelievers have targeted Muslim women, children, and elderly, it is permissible for Muslims to respond in kind and kill those similar to those whom the unbelievers killed."

- Civilians are in fact innocent but their killing is necessary to stop them from killing our innocents

  → killing of civilians *necessary*

Running through Osama bin Laden's texts is an insistence on reciprocity or symmetry: our people are innocent too. Of course, this argument gets blurred by his simultaneous indistinction between Western combatants and civilians. One can probably say that both sides fail to see the victims on the other side as persons but regard them as mere symbolic representations of the enemy. People only count their own dead. One should, of course, remember that the first and last theories of the killing of innocents, the theories of the unfortunate and the necessary, presuppose a distinction between guilty and innocent. So, within the indistinction, there are still distinctions.

Withdrawal for Security. Understandably, not much thought has been given to his repeated 'offers' of cease-fire. I am not, of course, suggesting or advocating a cease-fire dialogue with Al-Qaeda, but his proposals seem to corroborate with the analysis above that his primary goal is the liberation and reformation of Muslim countries.

On April 15 2004, he directed a "peace proposal" to "our neighbours north of the Mediterranean," in which he discusses the current security imbalance between the West and the Muslim countries: "It is well known that security is a vital necessity for every human being. We will not let you monopolize it for yourselves." He stresses his defensive response to atrocities committed by the West: "[o]ur actions are but a reaction to yours," saying further that they "only killed Russians after they invaded Afghanistan and Chechnya, we only killed Europeans after they invaded Afghanistan and Iraq, and we only killed Americans in New York after they supported the Jews in Palestine and invaded the Arabian peninsula, and we only killed them in Somalia after they invaded it in Operation Restore Hope."

Next, he asks the Europeans to consider: "In what creed are your dead considered innocent but ours worthless?" This is an argument for moral equality compared to what he sees as the West's moral hierarchization of the value of life. He then tries to appeal directly to the people of Europe, making a distinction first between the people and its rulers and then between Europe and the United States:

> If one looks at the murders that are still going on in our countries and yours, an important truth becomes clear, which is that we are both suffering injustice at the hands of your leaders, who send your sons to our countries, despite their objections, to kill and be killed. So it is in the interests of both sides to stop those who shed their own peoples' blood, both on behalf of narrow personal benefits and on behalf of the White House gang.

The solution to the reciprocal terror is for Europe to disengage from The US's war against Muslims: "[n]o sensible person would compromise his property, his security or his family just to please the liar in the White House." We must understand him as saying that there can be a local peace or ceasefire between Europe and Islam(ists):

> I call upon just men, especially scholars, media, and businessmen, to form a permanent commission to raise awareness among Europeans of the justice of our causes, primarily Palestine, making use of the enormous potential of the media. So I present to them this peace proposal, which is essentially a commitment to cease operations against any state that pledges not to attack Muslims or intervene in their affairs, including the American conspiracy against the great Islamic world. This peace can be renewed at the end of a government's term and the beginning of a new one, with the consent of both sides. It will come into effect on the departure of its last soldier from our lands, and it is available for a period of three months from the day this statement is broadcast.[104]

Here is an explicit link between war and occupation. Peace or ceasefire is conditional upon "the departure of its last soldier from our lands." We find

104. Bin Laden, "To the Peoples of Europe."

something similar in another proposal, this time from January 19 2006, where his "message to you is about the war in Iraq and Afghanistan and the way to end it." Again, he blames the West for the aggression and explains his own terror as defensive and reactive. He offers security in exchange of withdrawal: "If you have a genuine will to achieve security and peace, we have already answered you," meaning withdrawal for security. On the basis of this, a cease-fire could emerge allowing the two entities to co-exist: "[w] e do not object to a long-term truce with you on the basis of fair conditions that we respect . . . In this truce, both parties will enjoy security and stability and we will build Iraq and Afghanistan, which were destroyed by the war."[105]

Organization, network, symbol

In a conversation with Mark Juergensmeyer, retold in *Terror in the mind of God*, Hamas-leader Abdul Aziz Rantisi said that what separates Hamas from the PLO is that the PLO fights a national struggle, whereas Hamas fights a transnational struggle.[106] It's probably more correct to say that within the radical Islamist movement there is a dialectic between the national and the transnational struggle, just as there is between the religious and the political components of the doctrines and the fighting.

The important thing here is that radical Islamism, almost by necessity, has a global dimension (or has been brought thereto by the globalization of the war on terror causing a de-distinction between Islamist partisans and terrorists). This connects Al-Qaeda more to the anarchist than the partisan who doesn't tie his battle to the frame set by the state but ignores it as prioritized organizational form.[107]

This was a development already set out by Sayyid Qutb, explaining the global obligation of religion: "[i]t is not possible that Islam will confine itself to geographical boundaries, or racial limits, abandoning the rest of mankind and leaving them to suffer from evil, corruption and servitude to lords other than God almighty."[108] Religion introduces a non-geographical—ultimately universal—inclusion of humankind, dividing the world into believers and not-yet believers, which is why Qutb calls the revolution

105. Bin Laden, "Bin-bin Laden tape."
106. Juergensmeyer, *Terror in the Mind of God*, 214.
107. Thorup, "The Anarchist and the Partisan."
108. Qutb, *The Sayyid Qutb Reader*, 56

"not territorial but international." He lived in the pre-globalization era still caught in a national/international frame of thinking saying that "as a starter the members of the Muslim party, wherever they live, should focus on that place. Their eventual goal should, however, be a world revolution for the simple reason that any revolutionary ideology, which is humanity specific and seeking universal welfare, cannot reduce itself to a particular state or nation."[109]

Al Qaeda radicalized or globalized Qutb's internationalism. In the beginning, they were nationally grounded as *organizations* in Egypt, Saudi Arabia and Afghanistan but, with the declaration of a World Islamic Front for Jihad in February 1998, they morphed into a regional/global *network* and, after the US invasion of Afghanistan, the loss of bases and the emulation by various groups of al Qaeda's vision and strategy, into a truly global/universal *symbol*.[110] Each form is superimposed on the other, making al Qaeda an organization, a network and a symbol while also nationally, regionally and globally focused.

We can elaborate on the difference already worked out above and say that al Qaeda operates on two levels in regard to its goals. The first goal is religious or civilizational and it pits a global conflict between Islam and the West where the enemy is demonized and a general license to kill is declared. This defines al Qaeda as a radicalized liberation-partisan or, rather, a "world-aggressive revolutionary partisan."[111] But there is also another goal, more limited in scope, being political or geostrategic, and concerning the fight for Muslim independence on their own territories, which is a classic sovereignty issue. Here, a distinction is drawn between combatants and civilians and distinct demands are formulated (US troops out of Muslim lands), which, when fulfilled, would result in peace (or long term cease fire). This defines al Qaeda as an independence-partisan. The political goals parallel the classical partisan; a too narrow focus on the religious aspect, to the exclusion of all other elements, tends to misrepresent al Qaeda.

Continuing with the two kinds of struggle and enmities, and the state-centrist perspective, Islamist terror can be described as coming out of a state critique of the Muslim states and a perhaps anarchist-like kind of fighting by targeting heads of state coupled with a limited partisan goal of state conquest. This approach didn't succeed, as the failures in Egypt

---

109. Qutb, *The Sayyid Qutb Reader*, 64.

110. Gunaratna, "Terrorism in Southeast Asia," 420.

111. Schmitt, *Theorie des Partisanen*, 77.

(assassinations resulting in repression rather than revolution) testified to, and the more extended terrorist tactic was adopted along with a still more expansive critique and agenda. Islamist groups have usually fought in a classical guerrilla fashion. Their stated goals may have been Islamist but their prize was national: national liberation from what was perceived as either outside occupation or domestic despotism. The immediate and dominant goal was national; the global battle against The US or the West was a distant second. The primary objective was to (re)create a genuine Islamist rule in the Islamic countries which could then, perhaps, serve as mobilization point for the outer struggle against unbelief.

Osama bin Laden has consistently argued against this chain of operations. He wants to reverse it. His analysis is basically that The US is the force upholding the tyrants ruling Muslim countries and that Israel actively undermines all attempts at independence and strength on the Arabian Peninsula. The policy analysis, then, is like this:

1) The US out of all Muslim countries

2) Israel off the map

3) Reform of Muslim countries

The succession is not random.[112] The US is perceived as the main and essential backer of both Israel and the Muslim tyrants, just as Israel is seen as an all-important subversive force on the Arabian Peninsula. The analysis explains why all previous Islamist attacks and strategies have failed and it promises that the present struggle is not in vain. Destroy or weaken The US and both Israel and the tyrants will fall. Unlike what many seem to think, Osama bin Laden's analysis does not require the destruction or islamization of The US (Israel is a different story). In fact, there is little to support a theory of global domination. Even when he most explicitly makes it a religious eternal conflict, he seems more concerned to liberate Muslim lands than to conquer new ones. He perceives the battle between Islam and Christianity as 'just' a fact of the world. It doesn't have to compel land-grabbing.

Gilles Kepel explains the surge of islamist terror as the result of a terrorist learning process that abandoned the former Arab regime approach with attacks on the global state, USA: "[s]pectacular attacks on American, Israeli, or Western targets would resolve a major problem that had stymied

112. See al-Zawahiri's 2006 version of the plan in Stout et al., *The Terrorist Perspectives Project*, 139–40.

Islamist radicals for over a decade: their inability to mobilize popular support to overthrow established regimes and replace them with an Islamic state."[113] Michael Freeman agrees that "this controversial shift to attacking the 'far enemy' was largely due to the failure of the internal jihadis to achieve their aims in the face of the state response in places like Egypt and Algeria during the 1990s. Al Qaeda . . . was the primary actor responsible for this change of strategic focus."[114]

What seems to distinguish Islamist terrorism (at least in its Al-Qaeda variant) from the anarchist and partisan ones is the belief that *terror in itself can achieve victory*. Both the anarchist and the partisan (and the ideological terror of the 1960's and 1970's) saw terror as a preliminary tool before an actual mass-based uprising. But the Islamist terror is meant to do the job in itself, scaring the Americans into retreat and thereby causing the collapse of Israel and the puppet Arab regimes. If true, this would indicate a far more expansive use of terror, making groups like Al-Qaeda into pure terrorists making use of only terrorism from the rebellion arsenal.

A violence justified and criticized

Islamist terrorism projects a 'theology of power'[115] deliberately ignoring or belittling the peaceful teachings of Islam and exaggerating its belligerent parts. The past is reframed as one of constant battle. It's a militarization of Islam reducing religion to a confrontational power logic. This is an image reproduced by many Western observers, either in a total denunciation of Islam as totalitarian and violent throughout the ages, and for all Muslims, or in the description of Western societies as totally unprepared for the present onslaught threatening to extinguish our civilization. This mirror imagining of Islam as a warrior religion fighting one more battle against the infidels is bad thinking. It is bad theology and it is bad threat assessment.

Any argument, however dogmatically presented, invites counter-arguments. Al Qaeda is engaged in an armed battle with "the Crusader-Jewish Alliance" and its "Muslim puppet states." But they are also in a battle of ideas, having to justify their actions to various different audiences; to the believers in armed struggle about the correctness of their "far enemy"-approach and the wisdom of the 9/11-attacks; to Muslims in general about

113. Kepel, *The War for Muslim Minds*, 72.
114. Freeman, "Democracy, Al Qaeda," 42.
115. Charters, "Something Old. Something New," 74.

the use of violence, not least against fellow Muslims; and to a Western non-Muslim audience, trying to convince not about the righteousness of their struggle but the terrible consequences of not adhering to their demands.

Justifying violence is, at once, an easy task with many formulas readily available and also a difficult one because it leaves one open for attacks on one's morality. Claiming inaction as the immoral position may serve to stifle some dissent but killing and hurting others invariably provokes critique. In both the Islamist community and among Muslims in general, al Qaeda's actions have generated an increasing amount of critique. However much a violent actor rejects dialogue, the legitimacy of the violence opens one up for critique, especially when the promised rewards are not forthcoming. One must expect a growing rejection of the 'al Qaeda strategy' when—like in any organization or movement—victories and defeats are evaluated. There are already signs of this.[116] Al Qaeda not only generates opposition outside itself, that is to be expected, but it also creates antibodies from within: "[i]t generates its own counter-radicalization programme."[117] It doesn't necessarily mean a rejection of violence. It certainly doesn't mean an embrace of democracy. However, a counter-movement may be developing from within against al Qaeda's use of violence, started, ironically, because no political violence can take place today without the (by al Qaeda broken) promise of an anti-violent near future.

116. Wright, "The Rebellion Within."
117. Porter, "Long wars and long telegrams," 298.

6

Terror for Order: Right-wing Extremist Enmity

WE FREQUENTLY, AND QUITE naturally, view terrorists as violent actors wanting to create chaos and disorder. With their violence, however, most contemporary terrorists wish to create more order. They view the society at which they take aim as chaotic and disorderly. Terror serves in their view to clean up a depraved society and reinstall genuine order. This unites Islamic terrorists with the Norwegian right-wing extremist Anders Behring Breivik who killed 69 people on July 22, 2011.

16 years before that, immediately after the bombing of the Alfred Murrah building in Oklahoma City on April 19, 1995, where 168 people were killed by a car bomb, the American TV-commentator Steven Emerson said, "This was done with the intent to inflict as many casualties as possible. That is a Mideastern trait."[1] Shortly thereafter, it emerged that that the perpetrator was a white, Christian, American, Timothy McVeigh, whose motives came from right-wing extremism. Quite apart from the clear racism and lacking objectivity of Emerson's observation that the event had a 'Mideastern trait', it is interesting to note how today terrorist attacks are so quickly and automatically ascribed to radical Islam. When the first news of the Utøya-attack emerged, a Danish TV crime reporter Niels Brinch began by denying "the lone wolf" as the possible culprit and explained that it could only be related to Islamists.

---

1. Zulaika and Douglass, *Terror and Taboo*, 55.

The purpose here is not to criticize these automatic responses in pointing at culprits and motives.[2] There is a clear pattern in a whole series of gruesome acts of terror, going back well beyond this last decade. Instead, I offer an analysis of the possible links between the two, the accused culprit, the Islamic terrorist, and the actual culprit in Norway, the extreme right-wing terrorist, in that both are characterized by an exaggerated support for order. It is terror supporting order.

I do not want to suggest that all right-wing extremists are or become terrorists any more than one could say such nonsense about all Muslims or even Islamists. The vast majority of both groups avoids using violence and presumably do not condone it. What I do contend, however, is that there are a number of interesting and important parallels between the world-views of violent right-wing extremists and Islamists, not least their relation to the state and community that they are attacking. Significantly, they share common ways of thinking about order and disorder, leading some of them to tragic conclusions and actions.

We could have extended this comparison, taking account of radical religious traditions in Judaism, Hinduism, Christianity, and many others, but here—even if most of the right-wing extremist positions can be tracked back to (frequently distorted) Christian traditions—our focus remains on right-wing political extremism and political Islam. As I treated Islamic terrorism in the previous chapter, the primary aim of this chapter is analyzing and discussing extreme right-wing terror,[3] and here I will focus exclusively on the order aspect of the background and legitimation of extremist terrorism.

There has been some slightly bizarre cooperation between right-wing extremists and Islamists, as can be read in the book *The Enemy of my Enemy* by the American sociologist George Michael.[4] It is not my purpose to lay these tales bare. Nor do I wish to make more out of the two groups' normative links in their anti-modern advocacy of faith, nation, and family;

2. See Cole, "Top Ten Differences between White Terrorists and Others."

3. Literature on right-wing extremism, its violence and related themes is abundant. Good places to start are Merkl, *Political Violence and Terror*; Bjørgo and Witte, *Rasistisk vold i Europa*; Bjørgo, *Terror from the Extreme Right*; Kaplan and Bjørgo, *Nation and Race*; Kaplan and Lööw, *The Cultic Milieu*; Merkl and Weinberg, *Right-Wing Extremism in the Twenty-First Century*; Eatwell and Mudde, *Western Democracies and the New Extreme Right Challenge*.

4. Michael, *The Enemy of My Enemy*; Michael, "Michael Collins Piper"; Wright, "Strategic Framing of Racial-Nationalism." See also the very interesting reading of an anti-Western conceptual structure shared by both Western and non-Western traditions in Buruma and Margalit, *Occidentalism*.

in their opposition to the supposedly menacing dangers from secularism/ atheism, homosexuals, feminists, and global capitalism; nor will I discuss how the anti-Semitic extreme right-wing converges with the Islamists in their belief that Jews are behind all of the world's problems, this latter having been decisive for their cooperation in Holocaust-denial.

What I want to say instead is that there is a structural parallel between extreme right-wingers and Islamists with respect to the opponent they attack, which is the insufficient protector (the state) and the corrupt society (the population). There is as mentioned in the previous chapter, the assumption of treason as an explanation of the tendency of the Islamists and the extreme right-winger to inflict worse violence than other groups. It is important to note that in contrast to the extreme left-wing terrorism, as known from the Red Army Faction in Germany or the Red Brigades in Italy, the violence of both the Islamists and the extreme right wing is often directed not only at the representatives of the state but also at the civilian population.

This probably happens because the population is viewed as depraved (and not merely because they are misguided or suffering from a false consciousness as the left-wing terrorists assumed to a considerable degree). It is because of a sharing in the culpability of undermining the order which should otherwise prevail. This was, for instance, the case in England in 1999 where the Neo-Nazi David Copeland attacked what he viewed as a cancerous growth on the moral order (homosexuals) and the racial or religious order (Muslims). This led to three deaths and 130 wounded.

An idea is flourishing among commentators and academics that we face a form of 'new terrorism', and one of its characteristic traits is the mass murder of civilians, this being almost exclusively attributed to Islamist terrorists. In general, former day anarchist and extreme left-wing terrorism did not support or organize the mass murder of civilians. In contrast to this, right-wing extremists have been responsible for a number of successful and attempted cases of mass-murder, and some in the US have attempted to acquire weapons of mass destruction. We have mentioned Timothy McVeigh and one could also cite the bombing of Bologna's central station by a Neo-fascist group on August 2, 1980 where 85 people were killed and 200 wounded.[5]

This chapter is divided into five parts. The first introduces ideas about order and the second discusses how this order and the threats to it become

5. Ferraresi, *Threats to Democracy*.

the background for violence. The third section discusses some of the possible causes of this order fetishism shared by the extreme right-wing and
Muslims, while the fourth focuses on the Norwegian terrorist Anders
Breivik and his outlook on threats and traitors, with the fifth and final
section summarizing the thought processes of those who attack the very
societies and communities that they claim to want to protect.

Order+

Let us begin with a simple thesis about extreme right-wing terrorism. In
contrast to left-wing extremism, which seeks to undermine or replace the
existing order, right-wing extremism is generally characterized by an excessive approval of the existing order. Left-wing extremism 'lacks' loyalty
to the existing social order, whereas right-wing extremism has 'excessive'
loyalty to what it considers to be the principles of societal order.

Being schematically reductionist, you could say that this excessive
loyalty manifests itself in the religious order as fundamentalism (e.g.,
Iran, al-Qaeda, the anti-abortion killings in the US); in the statist order
as fascism (e.g., Mussolini's Italy); in the ethnic order as racism or Nazism
(e.g., Ku Klux Klan and Nazi Germany); in the political order as a military
coup (e.g., Pinochet in Chile); and in the patriarchal order as hyper male
chauvinism[6] and hatred of feminists and homosexuals. Behind these ideal
types lies a common obsession with the moral order that is understood as a
rampart holding off depravity and perversity.

Right-wing extremism is obsessively preoccupied with moral excesses
and the experience of violations of what they regard as the natural hierarchies and values. Fundamentalism is a reaction to the experience of violations of god's order. Fascism is a reaction to the experience of violations of
the state's sovereignty from within and without. Racism and Nazism are reactions to the perceived transgressions of racial hierarchies and the mixing
of populations. The right-wing oriented military coup is a reaction to the
experience of the failure of a political system to act in the face of subversive
elements, particularly from the left.[7] Hyper masculinity is a reaction to the
experience of the "feminization" of society, threatening to subvert men's
"natural" primacy.

6. Somewhat speculative but extremely interesting on the issue of fascism and male
chauvinism/ masculinity is Thewleit, *Male Fantasies*. For skinheads as 'warriors' see
Arena and Arrigo, *The Terrorist Identity*, chapter 9.

7. Thorup, *An Intellectual History of Terror*, chapter 11.

These reactions turn into right-wing extremist terrorism when the accumulation of violations of the natural order experienced become too abundant, and—which is completely decisive and diametrically opposed to extreme left-wing terrorism—when those who should otherwise protect the order do not respond in an appropriate fashion. Protection is then "privatized." It is exactly this *"privatization" of the protection of social order* that characterizes both extreme right-wing and Islamic terrorism.

Groups take it upon themselves to protect the threatened order, which is actually the state's responsibility, but which these groups claim the state neglects. In this sense, the designation "anti-government"—used with respect to Timothy McVeigh and Anders Breivik—is actually a misconception. The extreme right-wing is not against the state or government as such. They aim at having a state that acts like a state according to their way of thinking, protecting the greater social order in the sense of what religious, ethnic, political, etc. values might dominate their own particular orientation. Attacks against government buildings are thus not an expression of opposition to the government or the state, but rather a claim that the government itself is not acting as the government of a state should behave. Actually the attacks are a claim that it is the government that is anti-government or the state that is anti-state in their refusal to take on the alleged proper or vital tasks of state and government.

It is the government that does not behave as a good government, protecting its citizens against secularism, racial intermingling, the left-wing, etc. In McVeigh's justification for his act of terrorism, it emerges that it was "a retaliatory strike; a counter attack for the cumulative raids (and subsequent violence and damage) that federal agents had participated in over the preceding years." Referring to Waco, where the 51-day federal law enforcement siege in 1993 of a right-wing extremist group ended with the deaths of 76 people, McVeigh describes how the federal authorities "grew increasingly militaristic and violent, to the point where at Waco, our government—like the Chinese—was deploying tanks against its own citizens."[8] According to his own self-understanding, the attack was thus a defensive measure against a US state power that had transformed itself from the protector to the attacker.

---

8. McVeigh, "The McVeigh letters." See also Michel and Herbeck, *American Terrorist*. A brilliant examination of McVeigh's ideological milieu is Kaplan, "Right Wing Violence in North America."

If left-wing extremist terrorism is an assault on the existing order, then right-wing extremism is applied to support what one could call order+. This order+ is a confirmation of, and a support for, an order that goes significantly beyond that which the appointed or elected representatives of the order (the state, clerics, police, politicians, etc.) are ordinarily willing to go. And generally further than such representatives would understand as order of any kind.

In a reductionist fashion, one could state that the extreme left-wing has a tendency to attack *state power* (its buildings, institutions, and representatives), in contrast to which, the extreme right-wing and Islamic terrorism has a tendency to also or even primarily attack *civil society* (think about Anders Behring Breivik whose car bomb in the middle of the governmental quarter of Olso was "just" a distraction facilitating his actual attack against the politically oriented youth camp). In November 2012, the Swede Peter Mangs was found guilty of two cases of murder and four cases of attempted murder.[9] His goal would appear to have been racist and the victims of his shootings were ordinary private individuals selected in a completely arbitrary fashion.

About a decade and a half earlier, a similarly racist murderer, John Ausonius, otherwise known as the "laser man" spread death and mayhem in Stockholm in the early 1990s where he shot 11 people—one of whom died—most of them immigrants.[10] In Eastern Europe, Neo-Nazi attacks on Romani, Jews, immigrants, homosexuals, and other minorities are widespread. In Italy in 2011, an unknown individual with an automatic rifle shot and wounded 11 immigrants; an anti-racist organization registered 188 violent hate crimes (18 of which ended in deaths) in the first nine months of 2009.[11] In November 2011, the German Neo-Nazi group, the National Socialist Underground (NSU) was exposed. Since 2000, the group had murdered nine individuals with a migration background, as well as a policewoman, aside from robbing 14 banks and setting off a bomb in a Turkish quarter of Cologne wounding 22.[12]

Despite the differing focus, it is worth noting that while extreme left-wing terrorism rarely extends attacks to include ordinary individuals

9. Prasz, "Malmø-skytten får livstidsdom."

10. Dannemand, "Historien om lasermanden."

11. http://www.hrw.org/news/2011/03/21/italy-act-swiftly-end-racist-violence;   on racist violence in Italy, see http://www.hrw.org/node/97232.

12. http://www.spiegel.de/thema/braune_zelle_zwickau/.

(and where they have, they were almost always seen as representatives of state power such as the RAF abduction and later the liquidation of Hanns Martin Schleyer in 1977), extreme right-wing and Islamic terrorism is characterized by directing the main part of their violence at civil society itself and its member-groups. Admittedly, this can be extended to include those in power as in the case of the right-wing extremist Jared Lee Loughner in January 2011 when he killed 6 innocent people and injured another 14 including his actual target, representative Gabrielle Giffords in Tucson, Arizona.[13] This enlargement of the target focus is the concern of this chapter where the argument is that, as mentioned above, those organizing Islamic and more particularly extreme right-wing terrorism feel betrayed by the existing order and its representatives, an order they were supposed to feel protected by. To put it more pointedly: the representatives of the order are seen as being in league with, and protecting, the 'disorderly' member groups of society to which the violent groups are opposed. The existing order becomes a disorder, an order-dissolving entity. An attack on this disorder is, therefore, a confirmation of order, an order+.

Amuck for order

Right-wing extremism is all about the protection of that which is experienced as a menaced order, and extreme right-wing terrorism is violence on behalf of an order that is unwilling or incapable of protecting itself.

A couple of examples will suffice. Right-wing hooligans often describe themselves as the "true fans," "hard-core fans," or "ultras" in contrast to those who are only weakly connected to the local soccer club. They are not disturbed in their loyalty to the club by the fact that the club and its players criticize them, as their relationship to the club is a loyalty despite the club's official representatives whom they look upon with contempt in any case. The extreme right-wing means to protect the club, its honor and its order despite what the "official" club and the "official" fan club says. The ultra- and hard-core fans express precisely this excess in respect to the official club.

With its use of violence, the extreme right-wing loyalist terror group in Northern Ireland, the Ulster Defense Association, confirms its links to England, although the English state officially distances itself from them. An Ulster Protestant who had earlier served in the ordinary police of Northern Ireland, and later shifted to the terrorist group, said, "I got to the point

13. http://www.adl.org/PresRele/Extremism_72/5961_72.htm.

where I'd had enough so I resigned from the regiment. I joined the UDA for revenge and to take a real war to the IRA. We thought we could do it better than the security forces and we did."[14] He left the police which should have protected the protestant society of Northern Ireland in order to conduct a "real war." An imprisoned loyalist, Kenny McClinton, described this in a poem: "My country has abandoned me,/Tho' grizzly deeds I've done/For Ulsteder, so she might be free,/From Bomb and rebel's gun . . . Now Britain has imprisoned me,/A champion of her cause!/ And gives me weeks of solitary,/Like gifts from Santa Claus!"[15] Loyalty to the societal order literally demands violating "law and order" and leads to a powerful sense of betrayal among those who feel that they are fighting for the values of society.

Vigilante groups are a private "law enforcement" in the perceived absence of the state. The most familiar and paradigmatic examples are organized self-defense groups in the American Wild West (or in the South the original Ku Klux Klan; the theme has been developed by Hollywood in a series of films ranging from Dirty Harry to Batman). Self-defense usually begins as a private initiative (although there are countless examples of those which are either wholly or partly state-supported, such as the Argentinian Death Patrols, the Anti-Communist alliance)[16] to deal with an experience of disorder or insecurity, one with which the state either will not or cannot deal with:

> Vigilantism typically emerges in 'frontier' zones where the state is viewed as ineffective or corrupt, and it often constitutes a criticism of the failure of state machinery to meet the felt needs of those who resort to it. It is a form of self-help, with varying degrees of violence, which is activated *instead* of such machinery, against criminals and others whom the actors perceive as undesirables, deviants and 'public enemies.'[17]

In 1851, the self-defense group, The San Francisco Vigilante Committee proclaimed: "We are determined that no thief, burglar, incendiary, or

14. Wood, *Crimes of Loyalty*, 109.

15. Dillon, *God and the Gun*, 40. Also see the poem, 41-2 together with propaganda texts in Laqueur and Alexander, *The Terrorism Reader*, 134-137.

16. On state terror and state-sponsored terror, see Stohl and Lopez, *The State as Terrorist*; Rubin, *The Politics of Terrorism*; Perdue, *Terrorism and the State*; Pion-Berlin, *The Ideology of State Terror*; Claridge, "State Terrorism?"; Sproat, "Can the state commit acts of terrorism?"; Sluka, *Death Squad*; Campbell and Brenner, *Death Squads in Global Perspective*; Pilisuk and Wong, "State Terrorism"; Jackson, "The ghost of state terror."

17. Abrahams, *Vigilant Citizens*, 9.

assassin shall escape punishment either by quibbles of the law, the insecurity of prisons, the carelessness or corruption of police, or a laxity of those who *pretend* to administer justice."[18] This is the same logic that informs self-appointed, racist 'border patrols' on the Mexican-US border.[19]

The French OAS, a terror organization that fought to keep Algeria French and ended up pointing its weapons at the French state (having attempted, inter alia, to assassinate President de Gaulle), understood itself as defending France. One of its leaders, Gabriel Anglade said:

> We sought to remain French only because we deserved to be French. But France was not responsive to our desires. Our combat was simple: to keep Algeria as [three] départements of France. We were not predestined to be terrorists, but we had a mission—to defend the French flag. The Delta and colline units were composed of men who were prepared to die for their country. We are proud of what we did. Our dignity as Frenchmen would not permit us to act otherwise.[20]

The American anti-abortion terrorists claim to protect life that the state should protect, yet in fact themselves threaten and help to kill. The convicted anti-abortion terrorist and Christian fundamentalist Eric Rudolph, who killed two people and wounded 150, said, "I am not an anarchist. I have nothing against the government or the rule of law as such. It is only because this government has legalized the killing of children that I have no confidence in it, and deny the legitimacy of this specific government in Washington. Because I believe that abortion is murder, I also believe that violence is justified in the attempt to stop it." The American government does not protect those who are least capable of protecting themselves, the unborn, and thus private individuals should do so, according to Rudolph, and turn the aggression against the representatives of the government who are guilty of "mass murder, either consciously or unconsciously."[21]

In the same way, one can understand al Qaeda as motivated by despair that their political and religious leaders will not protect the full sovereignty of Muslim lands from the outside world, in particular against Western

18. Kirkpatrick, *Uncivil Disobedience*, 42, my italics.

19. Doty, "States of Exception on the Mexico-US Border: Security."

20. Harrison, *Challenging De Gaulle*, 73. See also Gaucher, *The Terrorists from Tsarist Russia to the OAS*, part 4.

21. http://www.armyofgod.com/EricRudolphStatement.html. See also Seegmiller, "Radicalized Margins."

influence and the American soldiers, and the internal moral purity (as documented in the previous chapter). Leaders who should protect society have revealed themselves to be attacking the people instead. Protectors have become the assailants and thus according to their own self-understanding, Al-Qaeda and other Islamic terror groupings have to attack the Muslim regimes (and peoples) in order to protect the people and the faith.

There is a clear tendency among both right-wing extremists and Islamists to attack the officially appointed protectors of social order because they are perceived as traitors against order and they have become the most important obstacle to a powerful affirmation and protection of that order. The Israeli scholar of the extreme-right, Ehud Sprinzak, wrote that in contrast to extreme left-wing groups that were directly opposed to the power of the state, for many right-wing religious and self-defense groups, this conflict is secondary, and that in principle, they assume that state power "is expected to cooperate or remain uninvolved."[22] However, this lack of conflict only applies as long as the power of the state is seen as a supporter, or at least as long as it does not prevent "solutions." If the state defends law and order against the self-appointed defenders of "social order," the state itself cannot be distinguished from the immediate enemy—the left, Muslims, Jews, atheists, homosexuals, etc. Or more accurately, the state becomes an instrument for achieving the enemy's agenda and the power of the state is transformed from a possible accomplice into one of the enemies. A process of radicalization takes place that arises from what Sprinzak called a "crisis of confidence," experienced by a group "whose confidence in the existing political government is greatly eroded."[23] This is the level of sporadic violence aimed at civil society groups, such as beating up homosexuals or leftists. When further radicalized, this shifts into a "conflict of legitimacy" that is "the behavioral stage that evolves when a challenge group, previously confined to criticizing the government, is ready to question the very legitimacy of the regime."[24] Here, a more systematic and ongoing violence is applied, the groups identifying themselves as those who commit violence, and this can lead to terrorism, the final stage of radicalization, termed a "crisis of legitimacy" which is:

> the behavioural and symbolic culmination of the two preceding stages. Its essence lies in the extension of the previous

22. Sprinzak, "Right-Wing Terrorism in a Comparative Perspective," 18
23. Ibid., 19
24. Ibid.

delegitimation of the system to *every individual* person associated with it. Individuals who are identified with the 'rotten' and 'soon to be destroyed' social and political order are depersonalized and dehumanized.[25]

Terroristic violence can now be unleashed, not only against the 'usual' groups of the socially despised, but also against all representatives of the system, since the system and all of its representatives, whether politicians, policemen, or others, are without exception linked to the system and dissolved as individuals, melting into the collective image of the enemy. It is at this point that Sprinzak calls it a *"dual process of delegitimatization"* that takes place, where there is an "intense delegitimization *vis-à-vis* the unaccepted non-governmental collectivity [social groups of, e.g., gays or Muslims] and a *diluted* delegitimization towards the regime."[26]

Broadly speaking, a common trait of right-wing extremist organizations is the claim of being betrayed by those who should be serving and protecting. This is probably an essential reason for right-wing extremism being quite consistently more violent than left-wing extremism. Nothing injures as much as treachery. By contrast, the theme of treachery is not deemed to be a major theme in left-wing extremism since, from the very beginning, the official representatives are viewed as protectors of an order that the attacking group does not recognize. You do not feel betrayed by someone who you do not expect anything from.

Thus, one can understand right-wing extremism as 'going amuck for order.' The rules and laws of the order can be broken because the extremist act in his or her transgression on behalf of that very same order (revealing a parallel to the 'torture for democracy'-argument), even up to that point when the appointed protectors of order become enemies themselves. For, the real and profound loyalty are not to the superficial and changing surface expressions of order, but rather to the intrinsic, immutable principles of that order. Therefore, the extremist can act against the contingent expressions on behalf of the underlying real and eternal order behind the present day depraved versions. The principles or the core values may be only weakly expressed in the official version of the social order as it exists—religion is the supporting principle for the fundamentalist social order, but it may be only a ritual detail in the official order; race or nation are real principles of life to racists, but the concepts may appear only tangentially in the official

25. Ibid., 20.
26. Ibid.

order as some kind of immigration policy, etc. In this situation, the extremist can be loyal to the order, but nevertheless attack it, since he or she is only attacking incidental, accidental, official, or unworthy representatives of the actual order that you are aiming to protect.

Chaos reigns

How can one explain this obsession with order? Why do right-wing extremists and Islamists share something that most people regard as being an exaggerated devotion to a principle of order sanctified?

In his book, *Holy Terror*, the Professor of English Literature, Terry Eagleton, writes that the absolutist or fundamentalist "whether Texas or Taliban, is the flipside of the nihilist." Both fundamentalists and nihilists or anarchists "believe that nothing has a meaning or value unless it is founded on cast iron first principles." Both "suspect that chaos is our natural condition. It is just that absolutists fear it, whereas anarchists revel in it."[27] Where the nihilist or anarchist want to further and live in chaos, the absolutist or fundamentalist fear that chaos, the dissolvement of all things holy, disorder lurking just beneath the surface of society; a constant possibility of the default position of society and humankind not constantly alert to the dangers. Humankind must be in chains or everyone will succumb to the temptations of chaos.

Eagleton divides the absolutists into the Texans (extreme right-wing) and the Taliban (Islamic) variants. They are constantly and terrifyingly preoccupied with all signs indicating a threat to undermine the holy, to infect or gnaw at the natural, that we are in the middle of a monstrous blend of the holy and the profane, the high and the low, the familiar and the alien, the natural and the unnatural, the pure and the impure, the exalted and the depraved. Both groups understand order as purity; chaos is mixing, indistinction, and blurring of the lines. This line of thinking turns to terrorist action when the conclusion is drawn that the end times are upon us, that a short window of opportunity is still open for action, that now is the last chance and then the designated protectors, whether the state, clerics, or leaders of whatever kind are rephrased from protectors to con-conspirators, 'useful idiots' or even outright attackers.

Right-wing extremists and Islamists absolutize order while anxiously fantasizing about the accelerating dissolution of society. Every deviation from the pure order leads only to total chaos, full dissolution and complete

27. Eagleton, *Holy Terror*, 26.

destruction. Right-wing extremists and Islamists share a train of thought that can only operate with absolutes: pure order or pure chaos. Order is understood as static (once established, it stands firm), while disorder is understood as degenerative (once it has begun, the dissolution accelerates on its own). Anarchy and perversion, mixing of what should be separate, contamination of the holy or the most fundamental principle, shifting the higher and the lower—all of this is for both the right-wing extremists and the Islamists the constantly existing possibility, possibly the always existing reality.

The left has a tendency to perceive the existence of social violence as contingent, i.e., a result of the actual acts and decisions of humans, and thus as something that can be remedied, and perhaps even eliminated through other acts. The right and particularly the extreme right version, share an understanding with the Islamists that the world is inherently violent. Violence is the result of human nature—and as with the fall from grace in Christianity, racial struggle in Nazism and others—it is thus an eternal state. The earth is strife and, therefore, there is a clear tendency to celebrate sacrifice, the mystery of death, martyrdom, warrior ideals, struggle as the meaning of life, and the like.[28] It is hardly accidental that Breivik perceived himself as a crusader. The world has, so they say, always been a violent place. In the end, order is only upheld through violence. Where the violent fantasies of the left-wing are revolution, i.e., a struggle to stand up to the power of the system, the right-wing dreams of civil war, i.e., a struggle turned inwards aimed at social life.

Anders Breivik and the war against the traitors

Breivik indisputably belongs to the extreme version of the modern anti-Muslim movement.[29] Much has been written about whether he is a racist, fascist, Nazi, culture conservative, or something fully new.[30] Part of the confusion is probably due to the fact that in his manifesto, Breivik himself is quite confused and contradictory on the matter himself. He shifts between subscribing to the traditional school of "classical" biological racism about the white race and its genetic degeneration, to "classical" fascism's position on the state's primacy over the individual, to "classical" patriotism's

28. Neocleous, "Long live death!"

29. For documentation of Breivik's initiation into the on-line anti-Islamic milieu, see Brown, "Anders Breivik's spider web of hate"; about the milieu see Expo, *Den antimuslimska miljön.*

30. Matzen, "Nyfascisten"; Harket, "Kulturkatastrofen."

attitude to the fatherland and faith, to "classical" hyper male chauvinism about the role of the man and the family and the dominance of hetero-sexuality, and finally to "classical" Nazism's stand on the national disloyalty of the Jews. However, all of this he jumbles together with a new form of ring-wing extremism that can be said to have replaced (a) the nation and (to a lesser degree) Christianity with Europe and the West; (b) race with culture; (c) anti-Semitism with anti-Islam and pro-Israeli sentiments; (d) the state with partnership; and (e) hyper male chauvinism with a "defense" of women and gay rights as opposed to the alleged "medieval values" of the Middle East. Breivik subscribes simultaneously to all these traditions and is thus a kind of anti-Hitler Nazi, anti-Semitic Zionist, Christian agnostic, Norway-indifferent nationalist, anti-feminist pro-abortion proponent of women's rights, anti-racist racist, etc. Should all this not force us to write off Breivik as nothing but the cold-blooded murderer that he so clearly is? Is there any argumentative substance or any kind of clear train of thought behind his actions?

There is, in fact, some kind of consistency in his train of thought and the supporting logic is exactly that of the treachery theme described here-inabove. Why attack a Scandinavian political youth camp and the Norwe-gian government district in red-hot hatred of everything Islamic, but not, e.g., a Muslim festival? Because the chief enemy is not the Muslim threat itself, but rather according to Breivik, those who have made the Muslim threat real, namely "the *landsmo(r)deren* [in Norwegian, you can use an additional letter to change "national mother" to "national murderer"] Gro Harlem Brundtland" [a former Labour prime minister] and the Norwe-gian Labour Party's support for "violent 'Stoltenberg Jugend'" [the word used in the text is the German from *Hitler Jugend* and not the Norwegian *Ungdom*, thus associating Norwegian Prime Minister Jens Stoltenberg with the Hitler Youth] who are those who "facilitate the Jihadists" and thus the main opposition—as Breivik wrote in a right-wing blog in January 2010 and October 2009, respectively.[31]

It is in this idea of being betrayed by his protectors, Breivik is united with bin Laden. This is not the place to analyze the various elements in his world view[32]—in particular his anti-feminism and thoughts on sexuality and his own family history appear to call out for examination. The prob-lem is that this risk becoming cheap psychoanalysis with commentaries

31. www.document.no/anders-behring-breivik/
32. Gardell, "The roots of Breivik's ideology"; Eriksen, "Hvad du ser i Breivik."

on women, feminism, reproduction, and homosexuality that are among the topics besides anti-Muslim sermonizing most repeatedly mentioned in the manifesto.[33] Moreover, his conspiracy theories and number fetishism likewise demand deeper investigations.

Breivik's manifesto is a 1,500 page long dream of civil war. The core of the problem is not the invasion of the Muslim hoards but a Western "lack of cultural self-confidence."[34] This is the result of the dominating trend of 'multiculturalism' and what he calls "cultural Marxism" which conceals truths, ridicules patriots, indoctrinates children, dissolves families, feminizes men, opens national boundaries, and permits all kinds of perversities. Multiculturalism—a blend of cultural Marxism and political correctness (described as the "EUSSR ideology," where the EU and the USSR are combined)—is "the root cause of the ongoing Islamisation of Europe which has resulted in the ongoing Islamic colonisation of Europe through demographic warfare (*facilitated by our own leaders*)."[35] These leaders are described as "cultural Marxists, suicidal humanists or capitalist globalisers" who have a "European hate ideology which was created to destroy our European cultures, national cohesion and Christendom (in other words Western civilisation itself)."[36] This hate ideology is "anti-God, anti-Christian, anti-family, anti-nationalist, anti-patriot, anti-conservative, anti-hereditarian, anti-ethnocentric, anti-masculine, anti-tradition, and anti-morality."[37]

The ruling ideology common to the political, economic, cultural, and intellectual elites, according to Breivik, is basically nothing but a continuous assault on the West from within. "We are slowly realising" he writes, "how our own elites have betrayed us and continue to do so." We thus stand in "the ongoing European civil war."[38] Breivik's manifesto and acts of terrorism are an attempt to make visible and clear for everyone else that which he sees as already a reality, namely a civil war; a civil war that the Western elites wage against their own peoples at the same time that they deny what is happening. Breivik's declared purpose was to bring to light what he thought already existed, but which would be perceived as reality later by

33. Gardell, "Antifeminism."
34. Breivik, *2083*, 11.
35. Ibid., 15; emphasis added.
36. Ibid., 365.
37. Ibid., 36.
38. Ibid., 730, 738.

all, as an armed and conscious confrontation of the nationalist versus the multicultural camps, rather than the continuous one-sided and undeclared process of cultural dissolution already in existence.

The third part of the manifesto, therefore, deals with what he calls a "a declaration of pre-emptive war" where he lays out his theory of the three different phases of the civil war, his thoughts about the new society, his self-glorification ("I am perhaps the biggest greatest champion of cultural conservatism, Europe has ever witnessed since 1950. I am one of many destroyers of cultural Marxism and as such; a hero of Europe, a savior of our people and of European Christendom—by default. A perfect example which should be copied, applauded and celebrated. The Perfect Knight I have always strived to be. A Justiciar Knight is a destroyer of multicultural-ism, and as such; a destroyer of evil and a bringer of light"),[39] the bomber's manual, journal and not least the fantasies of punishing his inner enemies. He made a list of different categories of traitors and measured out the punishments so that 400,000 Western Europeans should be executed for treason, whereas millions of others should be punished in other ways.[40] Total war on the inner total enemies in order to save the dream of an order thought disappearing before his very eyes.

Threatening (while "defending") the West

Whereas the Islamic terror at the beginning of this century was often represented as an existential threat, or even a civilizational menace to the West (which was certainly an exaggerated and twisted understanding of its dimensions), it is now clear that if there is a civilizational threat, it is from the extreme right. This is not because extreme right terror and violence can threaten the survival of Western society but because it is a violence that claims to act on behalf of the West, as a defense of the West even where—and even especially where—it is the Western institutions and citizens who are the victims of the assault.

In *The Year of Dreaming Dangerously*, the Slovenian philosopher Slavoj Žižek observed that in the spring of 2011, there were three gay parades in Istanbul, Belgrade, and Split, respectively. In Istanbul, the parade went peacefully, while the Serbian and Croatian parades were attacked by the far right, which was "defending" Christianity, morals, and the family. Žižek

---

39. Ibid., 1410. On his self-stylization see Behnke, "Dressed to kill. "
40. Breivik, *2083*, 918-920.

notes that it is these Western forms of "fundamentalists, not those of Tur-key [who] stand for the true threat to the European legacy."[41] Not because the threat of violence is enormous and greater than that of the Islamists, but rather because it is a violence—and a violence of critique—that comes from within, and twists the European heritage and identity to attack others.

Neo-Nazi skinheads, anti-Muslim terrorists, Christian fundamental-ists, the Orban-government in Hungary, the Golden Dawn fascist party in Greece with storm troopers in the streets—all are the "defenders" of the West, whose humanistic core values they attack. One can say that they split the European heritage: they fetishize the particular identity as a white man, European, Christian, patriotic, while at the same time expelling the same European identity's universal values united in the ideals of the En-lightenment and human rights.[42] Despite their wealth of words proclaim-ing substantial common and profound values, the "West" is reduced to an abstraction permitting the multi-faceted history of that very same West to be disavowed, condemning it to a (claustrophobic) uniformity. That is a uniformity falsified by European history and present reality, which is why the conceptual split becomes a more general division of the extreme right-winger between that West that actually exists and that West that the extreme right understands as the true West. The European heritage is thus reduced to the "lean and mean" version and transformed from an open and flexible identity to a communal defense society seeing enemies everywhere, leading some to conclude that attacking the actual existing residents of the West is the best defense of the dream of the "West."

41. Žižek, *The Year of Dreaming Dangerously*, 38.
42. Thorup, *Fornuftens perversion*.

Conclusion

Guide to Legitimate Violence (or Not)

THE TOTAL ENEMY IS not a break with modernity or its dirty secret. It is a radicalization of tendencies and explanatory models inherent in the anti-violence of modernity. The enemy becomes total because "they" emphatically stand in the way of realizing a world without violence. It is only—although you could see an early exemplar in the religious enmity of the Middle Ages—when you believe it to be within your power to shape history and control fate that the enemy can turn total because it is only then that you can make yourself believe that through the elimination of the total enemy a new society beyond violence, depravity, and injustice is born.

This book has been about some of the ways modern forms of enmity and violence turn total. However, the chapters also betray a viewpoint on enmity and violence that could be said to be modern politics as such, namely the naturalization of the state. The total as well as the terroristic, possibly even the violent, is very much coined in opposition to what is understood as statist normality; a normality that is so everyday and uncontested that it rarely even registers as a thing at all. By looking at Jacobins, terrorists of various sorts, Nazis both historical and contemporary, what tend to emerge, and what has emerged in this book, is a duality between those violent people and us; us meaning not only us as peoples or individuals but us as a state. Even when writing about a state, the totalitarian state in chapter 4, it inevitably serves to demarcate its difference to the liberal-democratic state. To write about violence is, as is profoundly also the case for the violent actors analyzed in this book, to see violence only on the other side.

A complementary book on modern forms of state enmities and violence turned total is perhaps needed to offset such an imbalance. Rather than that, and instead of a proper conclusion summarizing what has been learned from the preceding chapters, I offer a guide to legitimating violence. No author is in control of his or her text in the hands of readers, but I hope that it is evident that this guide is not meant to facilitate the guilt-free infliction of pain on others but rather to demonstrate what is, besides the historical claims of a particular modern assemblage of politics and language with enmity and violence, the main insight or claim of this book, namely that the legitimization of violence is a common "resource" and requirement for all violent actors and that the arguments, all other differences aside, are the same. There is such a thing as a modern language of violence. In this book, I have concentrated on historical steps in the emergence of that language (chapters 1 and 2) as well as radical expressions and uses of that language (chapters 3 to 6). Here, by way of concluding, I offer this guide as a way of demonstrating how none of us (other than infinitely few real-life pacifists) can escape the distinction between our violence to end all violence that is aimed at their violence to perpetuate more violence. The modern language of violence is anti-violence, because it must claim to halt a worse violence, but it is not necessarily any less violent.

Let us, finally, get to the practical side of the language of violence. If in need of legitimating political violence in public, use the following arguments:

Your violence is self-defense. Possibly the strongest argument for violence is defense of self, individually and collectively. As a Jewish rabbi explained the assassination of Israeli Prime Minister Rabin: "If you are convinced another Holocaust is coming . . . then you can come to the conclusion that it's all right to murder someone to stop it."[1] Remember: when under attack, violence may be not only necessary but the only moral course of action. This ensures that:

Your violence is a response to theirs. Don't be afraid of "they started it" arguments. For your violence to be legitimate, violence must have already been committed. A situation of violence, war, conflict, or ongoing repression has to exist so that you merely respond to it, seeing that there is no other option. Devote considerable attention to establish and document a

---

1. Alianak, "Mentality of Messianic Assassins."

"violent situation," that is, an argument of an existing violence that you seek to address because:

Your violence will lead to less violence. Any justification of violence has to entail the promise of the expulsion of violence from your community. Violence must serve anti-violence. Explain why non-action, non-violence, will lead to the continuation or even better escalation of violence and substantiate how your action promises to halt that violence. This can be achieved because:

You are peace, and your enemy is violence. Be careful not to be associated with or identified by your violence. Portray yourself as completely without any essential relation to the violence that you commit; violence that you are tragically and unwillingly compelled to use. Your enemy, on the other hand, must be portrayed as violence incarnate. Violence is not merely their way of operating. It is their very being. Continuous violence is intimately at the core of their existence in this world, whereas your violence is accidental to your being and occasional in its use. Use words to the effect that you are not your violence and associate your enemy's selfhood with pure, unmotivated violence. To achieve that, it helps to explain that your violence gives you:

No personal gain. Political violence can only serve universal, not particularistic, goals. Feel free to mention how you are protecting your own community (remember the self-defense argument) but make sure to do just as the Western heads of state did during the Kosovo conflict: "This is not a war for territory but a fight for values." Emphasize how your violence serves the world community rather than only your own; how it protects the innocents and upholds the universal values of human rights. Deny all allegations that it serves your own, particularistic economic or political interests. Portray yourself as merely the tool of universality. Use the terms "values," "human rights," "humanity," "world peace," "protecting civilians," etc. Your violence is in the service of the universal whether that is the nation, freedom, civilization, creed, the globe, etc. The larger the better. The actions that could be described as violence, murder, attack, terrorism, and plunder can now be redescribed as allegiance to higher values and as a form of piety. Connected to this point is the imperative of:

No joy. Remember that "losing control" is the bad excuse of an individual, not of a collective. The same goes for any display of excitement about your violence. Emphasize the calm and thorough deliberations that led to the decision to use violence. Deny any hatred or revenge motives as it individualizes and emotionalizes your justification, making you one with your violence. Use words such as "careful deliberation," "calculation," and other detached, rational terms. To disassociate yourself further from your violence, also emphasize that this is your:

Last resort. Violence must never be your first option. It is paramount to demonstrate how you have exhausted all other options, appealed to your enemy's (albeit diminished) rationality and humanity and only use violence out of pure, final necessity. Use different variations of "Violence is unfortunately the only language they understand," "We have tried every other way," and "We can no longer just sit and wait." It helps to insert an arbitrary time frame to make it imperative to act now, making it obvious that all other options are rapidly becoming obsolete. Remember:

Their barbarism is your mandate to act. As the Rote Armee Faction violent actor Gudrun Ensslin said: "This fascist state means to kill us all. We must organize resistance. Violence is the only way to answer violence. This is the Auschwitz generation and there's no arguing with them."[2] When your enemy is pure violence (the Nazi reference is always effective) they will, of course, only respond to violence. Furthermore, consider the violent potentials in this way of arguing from an American general during the 1990 Iraq war: "If I could have killed every Iraqi in Kuwait City, I would have . . . I went after that convoy primarily because of the barbaric and ruthless way they had treated people in Kuwait. There were no worse people on the face of the earth."[3] The more evil and barbaric your enemy can be made to look the freer hands you have to inflict serious pain without objections raised. To sustain the distinction, a hedging of your violence (or the appearance thereof) is needed, so:

No excess violence. Your violence exists to reduce violence in the world, making all excess violence highly problematic. Emphasize and document all attempts to minimize civilian casualties, mention your strict upholding of the rules of combat and the laws of war. Say "international conventions," "minimal force necessary," "smart bombs," "precision," etc. and highlight the difference between your discriminatory use of violence and your enemy's indiscriminate, random killings. Work the dichotomies between war/war crimes, liberation struggle/terrorism, and self-defense/vigilantism to your advantage. To do that:

2. Joanne Wright, *Terrorist Propaganda*, 110.
3. Campbell, *Politics without Principle*, 70.

Exploit historical parallels. The past is history and will not complain. Use historical parallels to guide your audience to the proper conclusion about the necessity of violence. World War I and II are always exploitable for a "good war" narrative and to paint your enemy in the colors of barbarism. Use sentences such as "We have seen this evil before," "History teaches us . . . ," or the all-time favorite "the new Hitler." By using the proper historical parallels you also indicate that while they attacked us we will prevail in the end and restore our glory through violence. Finally:

Describe your violence as something other than just violence. It is imperative that you verbalize your violence as anything but evil and brute force. Use "necessity," "defense," "humanitarian intervention," "anti-terrorism," "love" even, and remember: violence is what the others do and what you react against. Learn from the masterly narrative of Nelson Mandela during his 1964 trial:

> I do not, however, deny that I planned sabotage. I did not plan it in a spirit of recklessness, nor because I have any love of violence. I planned it as a result of a calm and sober assessment of the political situation that had arisen after many years of tyranny, exploitation, and oppression of my people by the Whites. . . . Firstly, we believed that as a result of Government policy, violence by the African people had become inevitable, and that unless responsible leadership was given to canalize and control the feelings of our people, there would be outbreaks of terrorism which would produce an intensity of bitterness and hostility between the various races of this country which is not produced even by war. Secondly, we felt that without violence there would be no way open to the African people to succeed in their struggle against the principle of white supremacy. All lawful modes of expressing opposition to this principle had been closed by legislation, and we were placed in a position in which we had either to accept a permanent state of inferiority, or to defy the Government. We chose to defy the law. We first broke the law in a way which avoided any recourse to violence; when this form was legislated against, and then the Government resorted to a show of force to crush opposition to its policies, only then did we decide to answer violence with violence.
>
> But the violence which we chose to adopt was not terrorism. We who formed Umkhonto were all members of the African National Congress, and had behind us the ANC tradition of non-violence and negotiation as a means of solving political disputes. We believe that South Africa belongs to all the people who live in it, and not to one group, be it black or white. We did not want an

> interracial war, and tried to avoid it to the last minute. . . . It was
> only when all else had failed, when all channels of peaceful protest
> had been barred to us, that the decision was made to embark on
> violent forms of political struggle . . . in view of this situation I have
> described, the ANC was prepared to depart from its fifty-year-old
> policy of non-violence to this extent that it would no longer disap-
> prove of properly controlled violence. . . . Experience convinced us
> that rebellion would offer the Government limitless opportunities
> for the indiscriminate slaughter of our people. But it was precisely
> because the soil of South Africa is already drenched with the blood
> of innocent Africans that we felt it our duty to make preparations
> as a long-term undertaking to use force in order to defend our-
> selves against force.[4]

It may seem odd or rude to end a book on the total enemy with a long quote by the political leader of "the total 20th century" most explicitly advocating what we could term a detotalizing enmity. Mandela activated the language and practice of political violence, but confronted with a regime deserving of the condemnation as a total enemy not only of black South Africans but of humanity and confronting those in his camp advocating total enmity against not only the regime but the whites, in general (as evident from Zim-babwe), Mandela managed to keep the enmity present and active while not succumbing to the seductions of the total enmity. This quote from Mandela shows us that not only the worst of us but also the most saintly among us all are implicated in the same moral reasoning when contemplating violence. It may be, as it often is, poor logic and immoral reasons, but it is moral reasoning all the same. And that moral reasoning can lead you all the way to the total enemy where only the death of the despised other will suffice.

Let us not forget that Mandela and the ANC were subjected to the total enmity of not only the Apartheid regime but also from its various Western cheerleaders, like the British Conservative Student's Union who in the 1980s had a poster with a grainy photo of Mandela and the caption: "Hang Nelson Mandela and *all* ANC terrorists: They are butchers," hereby stupidly but perfectly summarizing the logic behind the total enemy and the violence it brings.

4. Mandela, "I am prepared to die."

Bibliography

Abrahams, Ray. *Vigilant Citizens: Vigilantism and the State*. Cambridge: Polity, 1998.

Agamben, Giorgio. *Homo Sacer*. Stanford: Stanford University Press, 1998.

———. *Means without End*. Minneapolis: University of Minnesota Press, 2000.

———. *Remnants of Auschwitz*. New York: Zone, 2002.

———. *State of Exception*. Chicago: University of Chicago Press, 2005.

Alianak, Sonia L. "Mentality of Messianic Assassins." *Orbis* 44 (2000) 283–95.

Al Qaeda. "Statement from qaidat al-jihad regarding the mandates of the heroes and the legality of the operations in New York & Washington", 2002. Online: www.mepc.org/journal_vol10/alqaeda.html.

Andersen, Lars Erslev. *Innocence Lost: Islamism and the Battle over Values and World Order*. Odense: University Press of Southern Denmark, 2007.

Andress, David. *The Terror: Civil War in the French Revolution*. London: Abacus, 2006.

Anonymous. *Through Our Enemies' Eyes: Osama bin Laden, Radical Islam, and the Future of America*. Washington, DC: Brassey's, 2002.

Arblaster, Anthony. *The Rise and Decline of Western Liberalism*. Oxford: Basil Blackwell, 1984.

Arena, Michael P., and Bruce A. Arrigo. *The Terrorist Identity: Explaining the Terrorist Threat*. New York: New York University Press, 2006.

Arendt, Hannah. "Approaches to the German Problem." In *Essays in Understanding*, 106–20. New York: Shocken, 1993 [1945].

———. "Mankind and Terror." In *Essays in Understanding*, 297–306. New York: Shocken, 1993 [1953].

———. *On Revolution*. London: Penguin, 1965.

———. *Origins of Totalitarianism, vol. I: Antisemitism*. New York: Shocken, 2004 [1967].

———. *Origins of Totalitarianism, vol. II: Imperialism*. New York: Shocken, 2004 [1967].

———. *Origins of Totalitarianism, vol. III: Totalitarianism*. New York: Shocken, 2004 [1967].

———. "We Refugees." In *The Jew as Pariah*, 55–66. New York: Shocken, 1978 [1943].

———. "What remains? The Language Remains: A Conversation with Günter Grass." In *Essays in Understanding*, 1–23. New York: Shocken, 1993 [1964].

Aron, Raymond. *Clausewitz. Philosopher of War*. London: Routledge & Kegan Paul, 1983 [1976].

———. *Democracy and Totalitarianism*. London: Weidenfeld & Nicolson, 1968 [1965].

Baczko, Bronislaw. *Ending the Terror: The French Revolution after Robespierre*. Cambridge: Cambridge University Press, 1994.

Baehr, Peter. "Max Weber and the Avatars of Caesarism." In *Dictatorship in History and Theory*, edited by Peter Baehr & Melvin Richter, 155–74. Cambridge: Cambridge University Press, 2004.

Bates, David W. "Enemies and Friends: Arendt on the imperial republic at war." *History of European Ideas* 36 (2010) 112–24.

———. *Enlightenment Aberrations. Error & Revolution in France*. Ithaca: Cornell University Press, 2002.

Battersby, Christine. "Terror, terrorism and the sublime: rethinking the sublime after 1789 and 2001." *Postcolonial Studies* 6 (2003) 67–89.

Bauman, Zygmunt. *Modernity and Holocaust*. Cambridge: Polity, 1989.

Beetham, David. "From Socialism to Fascism: The Relation between Theory and Practice in the Work of Robert Michels. II. The Fascist Ideologue." *Political Studies* 25 (1977) 161–81.

Behnke, Andreas. "Dressed to kill. The sartorial code of Anders Behring Breivik." In *Terrorist Transgressions. Gender and the Visual Culture of the Terrorist*, edited by Sue Malvern and Gabriel Koureas, 137–56. London: I.B. Taurus, 2014.

Beinin, Joel, and Joe Stork, eds. *Political Islam. Essays from the Middle East Report*. New York: I.B. Tauris, 1997.

Bellamy, Richard. "The advent of the masses and the making of the modern theory of democracy." In *The Cambridge History of Twentieth-Century Political Thought*, edited by Terence Ball & Richard Bellamy, 70–103. Cambridge: Cambridge University Press, 2003.

Bergen, Peter L. *Holy War, Inc. Inside the Secret World of Osama bin Laden*. New York: Free Press, 2001.

Bernstein, Richard. "Hannah Arendt on the Stateless." *Parallax* 11 (2005) 46–60.

Bessner, Daniel, and Michael Stauch. "Karl Heinzen and the Intellectual Origins of Modern Terror." *Terrorism and Political Violence* 22 (2010) 143–76.

Bienvenu, Richard, ed. *The Ninth of Thermidor: The Fall of Robespierre*. New York: Oxford University Press, 1968.

Bin Laden, Osama. "Among A Band of Knights, February 14, 2003." In *Messages to the World: The Statements of Osama bin Laden*, edited by Bruce Lawrence, 186–206. New York: Verso, 2005.

———. "Bin-Laden tape, January 19, 2006." Online: http://newsvote.bbc.co.uk.

———. "Bin Ladin audiotape attacking Muslim scholars, July 7, 2003." In *Al-Qaida Statements 2003–2004*, edited by Thomas Hegghammer, 33–8. Online: http://rapporter.ffi.no/rapporter/2005/01428.pdf.

———. "Declaration of Jihad, August 23, 1996." In *Dokumentasjon om al-Qaida - intervjuer, kommunikéer og andre primærkilder, 1990–2002*, edited by Thomas Hegghammer, 123–41. Online: http://rapporter.ffi.no/rapporter/2002/01393.pdf.

———. "Depose the Tyrants, December 16, 2004." In *Messages to the world. The Statements of Osama bin Laden*, edited by Bruce Lawrence, 245–75. New York: Verso, 2005.

———. "Fight On, Champions of Somalia, March 19, 2009." Online: http://www.nefafoundation.org/miscellaneous/nefaublo309-2.pdf.

———. "From Somalia to Afghanistan, March 1997." In *Messages to the World: The Statements of Osama bin Laden*, edited by Bruce Lawrence, 44–57. New York: Verso, 2005.

————. "Interview with al-Jazira, 1999." In *Dokumentasjon om al-Qaida - intervjuer, kommunikéer og andre primærkilder, 1990-2002*, edited by Thomas Hegghammer, 69–76. Online: http://rapporter.ffi.no/rapporter/2002/01393.pdf.

————. "Interview with Jamal Isma'il, al-Jazira, December 22, 1998." In *Dokumentasjon om al-Qaida - intervjuer, kommunikéer og andre primærkilder, 1990-2002*, edited by Thomas Hegghammer, 50–53. Online: http://rapporter.ffi.no/rapporter/2002/01393.pdf.

————. "Interview with John Miller, ABC News, December 24, 1998." In *Dokumentasjon om al-Qaida - intervjuer, kommunikéer og andre primærkilder, 1990-2002*, edited by Thomas Hegghammer, 56–69. Online: http://rapporter.ffi.no/rapporter/2002/01393.pdf.

————. "Interview with Robert Fisk, The Independent, July 10, 1996." In *Dokumentasjon om al-Qaida - intervjuer, kommunikéer og andre primærkilder, 1990-2002*, edited by Thomas Hegghammer, 38–9. Online: http://rapporter.ffi.no/rapporter/2002/01393.pdf.

————. "Message to the Islamic Nation on 60th Anniversary of Israel, May 18, 2008." Online: http://www.nefafoundation.org/miscellaneous/FeaturedDocs/nefabinladen0508-2.pdf.

————. "Nineteen Students, December 26, 2001." In *Messages to the World: The Statements of Osama bin Laden*, edited by Bruce Lawrence, 145–57. New York: Verso, 2005.

————. "Osama bin Laden. Interview by Robert Fisk, December 6, 1996." Online: www.robert-fisk.com/usama_bin_ladin_in_sudan1996.htm.

————. "Osama bin Laden on al-Jazira, November 3, 2001." In *Dokumentasjon om al-Qaida - intervjuer, kommunikéer og andre primærkilder, 1990-2002*, edited by Thomas Hegghammer, 155–9. Online: http://rapporter.ffi.no/rapporter/2002/01393.pdf.

————. "Osama bin Laden on al-Majalla, October 27, 2002." In *Dokumentasjon om al-Qaida - intervjuer, kommunikéer og andre primærkilder, 1990-2002*, edited by Thomas Hegghammer, 185–7. Online: http://rapporter.ffi.no/rapporter/2002/01393.pdf.

————. "Practical Steps to Liberate Palestine, March 14, 2009." Online: http://www.nefafoundation.org/miscellaneous/FeaturedDocs/nefaublo309.pdf.

————. "Quagmires of the Tigris and Euphrates, October 19, 2003." In *Messages to the World: The Statements of Osama bin Laden*, edited by Bruce Lawrence, 207–11. New York: Verso, 2005.

————. "Resist the New Rome, January 4, 2004." In *Messages to the World: The Statements of Osama bin Laden*, edited by Bruce Lawrence, 212–32. New York: Verso, 2005.

————. "Terror for Terror, October 21, 2001." In *Messages to the World: The Statements of Osama bin Laden*, edited by Bruce Lawrence, 106–29. New York: Verso, 2005.

————. "The Betrayal of Palestine, December 29, 1994." In *Messages to the World: The Statements of Osama bin Laden*, edited by Bruce Lawrence, 3–14. New York: Verso, 2005.

————. "The Example of Vietnam, November 12, 2001." In *Messages to the World: The Statements of Osama bin Laden*, edited by Bruce Lawrence, 139–44. New York: Verso, 2005.

————. "The Towers of Lebanon, October 29, 2004." In *Messages to the World: The Statements of Osama bin Laden*, edited by Bruce Lawrence, 237–44. New York: Verso, 2005.

————. "The Winds of Faith, October 7, 2001." In *Messages to the World: The Statements of Osama bin Laden*, edited by Bruce Lawrence, 103–5. New York: Verso, 2005.

―――. "The World Islamic Front, February 23, 1998." In *Messages to the World: The Statements of Osama bin Laden*, edited by Bruce Lawrence, 58–62. New York: Verso, 2005.

―――. "To the Allies of America, November 12, 2002." In *Messages to the World: The Statements of Osama bin Laden*, edited by Bruce Lawrence, 173–75. New York: Verso, 2005.

―――. "To the Americans, October 6, 2002." In *Messages to the World: The Statements of Osama bin Laden*, edited by Bruce Lawrence, 160–72. New York: Verso, 2005.

―――. "To the People of Iraq, February 11, 2003." In *Messages to the World: The Statements of Osama bin Laden*, edited by Bruce Lawrence, 179–85. New York: Verso, 2005.

―――. "To the Peoples of Europe, April 15, 2004." In *Messages to the World: The Statements of Osama bin Laden*, edited by Bruce Lawrence, 233–36. New York: Verso, 2005.

―――. "To our brothers in Pakistan, September 24, 2001." In *Messages to the World: The Statements of Osama bin Laden*, edited by Bruce Lawrence, 100–102. New York: Verso, 2005.

―――. "Usama bin Laden: Interview with 'Dawn' and 'Ausaf', November 9, 2001." Online: www.robert-fisk.com/usama_interview_hamid_mir_ausaf.htm.

―――. "Usama bin Laden Says Al-Qaʻidah Group had Nothing to Do with the 11 September Attacks, September 28, 2001." Online: www.robert-fisk.com/usama_interview_ummat.htm.

―――. "Wrath of God. Interview of Osama bin Laden by Rahimullah Yusufzai, January 11, 1999." Online: www.time.com/time/asia/asia/magazine/1999/990111/osama1.html.

Bjørgo, Tore, ed. *Terror from the Extreme Right*. London: Frank Cass, 1995.

―――, and Rob Witte, eds. *Rasistisk vold i Europa*. Oslo: Tiden, 1993.

Brancaforte, Charlotte L., ed. *The German Forty-Eighters in the United States*. New York: Peter Lang, 1989.

Breivik, Anders Behring. *2083: A European Declaration of Independence*. 22 July 2011. Online: https://www.fas.org/programs/tap/_docs/2083_-_A_European_Declaration_of_Independence.pdf.

Breuer, Stefan. "Nationalstaat und pouvoir constituant bei Sieyes und Carl Schmitt." *Archiv für Rechts- und Sozialphilosophie* 70 (1984) 495–517.

Brisard, Jean-Charles. *Zarqawi. The New Face of al-Qaeda*. Cambridge: Polity, 2005.

Brooke, Steven. "Jihadist Strategic Debates before 9/11." *Studies in Conflict & Terrorism* 31 (2008) 201–26.

Buck-Morss, Susan. *Thinking Past Terror: Islamism and Critical Theory on the Left*. New York: Verso, 2003.

Burke, Edmund. "A Letter to a Member of the National Assembly." In *Edmund Burke: Selected Speeches and Writings*, edited by Peter J. Stanlis, 609–22. London: Transaction, 2006 [1791].

―――. "First Letter on a Regicide Peace." In *Empire and Community: Edmund Burke's Writings and Speeches on International Relations*, edited by David P. Fidler and Jennifer M. Welsh, 287–320. Oxford: Westview, 1999 [1776].

―――. "Fourth Letter on the Regicide Peace: To the Earl of Fitzwilliam." In *The Works of Edmund Burke*, 319–405. London: The World's Classics, vol. 6, 1906 [1797].

―――. *Reflections on the Revolution in France*. London: Penguin, 1968 [1790].

———. "Remarks on the Policy of the Allies." In *Empire and Community: Edmund Burke's Writings and Speeches on International Relations*, edited by David P. Fidler and Jennifer M. Welsh, 264–86. Oxford: Westview, 1999 [1793].

———. "Second Letter on the Regicide Peace: On the Genius and Character of the French Revolution as it regards other Nations." In *The Works of Edmund Burke*, 176–210. London: The World's Classics, vol. 6, 1906 [1797].

———. "Speech on American Taxation." In *Empire and Community: Edmund Burke's Writings and Speeches on International Relations*, edited by David P. Fidler and Jennifer M. Welsh, 100–18. Oxford: Westview, 1999 [1774].

———. "Third Letter on the Regicide Peace: On the Rupture of the Negotiation; the Terms of Peace Proposed; and the Resources of the Country for the Continuance of the War." In *The Works of Edmund Burke*, 211–318. London: The World's Classics, vol. 6, 1906 [1797].

———. "Thoughts on French Affairs." In *Empire and Community: Edmund Burke's Writings and Speeches on International Relations*, edited by David P. Fidler and Jennifer M. Welsh, 236–53. Oxford: Westview, 1999 [1791].

———. "Thoughts on the Cause of the Present Discontents." In *Edmund Burke: Selected Speeches and Writings*, edited by Peter J. Stanlis, 121–75. London: Transaction, 2006 [1770].

Buruma, Ian, and Avishai Margalit. *Occidentalism. The West in the Eyes of its Enemies*. New York: Penguin, 2004.

Bush, George W. "President Bush Calls on Congress to Act on Nation's Priorities, September 23, 2002." Online: www.whitehouse.gov/news/releases/2002/09/print/20020923-2.html.

———. "President: We're Fighting to Win – And Win We Will, December 7, 2001." Online: www.whitehouse.gov/news/releases/2001/12/print/20011207.html.

———. "Presidential Address to the Nation, October 7, 2001." Online: www.whitehouse.gov/news/releases/2001/10/print/20011007-8.html.

———. "Remarks by the President Upon Arrival, September 16, 2001." Online: www.whitehouse.gov/news/releases/2001/09/print/20010916-2.html.

———. "Statement by the President in His Address to the Nation, September 11, 2001." Online: www.whitehouse.gov/news/releases/2001/09/print/20010911-16.html.

Boffa, Massimo. "Counter-revolution." In *A Critical Dictionary of the French Revolution*, edited by Francois Furet and Mona Ozoud, 640–48. Cambridge, MA: Belknap, 1989.

Brown, Andrew. "Anders Breivik's spider web of hate." *The Guardian*, 7 September 2011.

Brown, Howard G. *Ending the French Revolution. Violence, Justice and Repression from the Terror to Napoleon*. Charlottesville: University of Virginia Press, 2006.

Burney, John M. "The fear of the executive and the threat of conspiracy: Billaud-Varenne's terrorist rhetoric in the French revolution, 1788–1794." *French History* 5 (1991) 143–63.

Calvert, Peter. "Terror in the Theory of Revolution." In *Terrorism, Ideology and Revolution*, edited by Noel O'Sullivan, chapter 2. Brighton: Wheatsheaf, 1986.

Campbell, Bruce B., and Arthur. D. Brenner. *Death Squads in Global Perspective: Murder with Deniability*. London: Macmillan, 2000.

Campbell, David. *Politics Without Principle: Sovereignty, Ethics, and the Narrative of the Gulf War*. Boulder: Lynne Rienner, 1993.

Camus, Albert. *The Rebel: An Essay on Man in Revolt*. New York: Vintage, 1957.

Chaliand, Gérard and Arnaud Blin, eds. *The History of Terrorism from Antiquity to al Qaeda.* Berkeley: University of California Press, 2007.

Charters, David A. "Something Old. Something New . . . ? Al Qaeda, Jihadism, and Fascism." *Terrorism and Political Violence* 19 (2007) 65–93.

Claridge, David. "State Terrorism? Applying a definitional model." *Terrorism and Political Violence* 8 (1996) 47–63.

Cole, Juan. "Top Ten Differences between White Terrorists and Others," 8 September 2012. Online, http://www.juancole.com/2012/08/top-ten-differences-between-white-terrorists-and-others.html.

Cozzens, Jeffrey B. "Approaching al-Qaeda's warfare: function, culture and grand strategy." In *Mapping Terrorism Research. State of the art, gaps and future direction*, edited by Magnus Ranstorp, chapter 7. London: Routledge, 2007

Cristi, Renato. "Carl Schmitt on Sovereignty and Constituent Power." In *Law as Politics - Carl Schmitt's Critique of Liberalism*, edited by David Dyzenhaus, 179–95. London: Duke University Press 1988.

Cruickshank, Paul and Mohannad Hage Ali. "Abu Musab Al Suri: Architect of the New Al Qaeda." *Studies in Conflict & Terrorism* 30 (2007) 1–14.

Dangerfield, George. *The Strange Death of Liberal England.* London: Paladin, 1970 [1935].

Dannemand, Henrik. "Historien om lasermanden." *Berlingske Tidende*, 13 February 2007.

Davies, Peter. *Extreme Right in France, 1789 to the Present.* New York: Routledge, 2002.

Derrida, Jacques. *The Beast and the Sovereign I.* Chicago: University of Chicago Press, 2009.

Dillon, Martin. *God and the Gun. The Church and Irish Terrorism.* London: Orion, 1998.

Doty, Roxanne Lynn. "States of Exception on the Mexico-US Border: Security, 'Decisions', and Civilian Border Patrols." *International Political Sociology* 1 (2007) 113–37.

Edelstein, Dan. "The Law of 22 Prairial: Introduction." *Telos* (2007) 82–91.

Eagleton, Terry. *Holy Terror.* Oxford: Oxford University Press, 2005.

Eatwell, Roger, and Cas Mudde, ed. *Western Democracies and the New Extreme Right Challenge.* London: Routledge, 2004.

Elias, Norbert *The Civilizing Process.* Oxford: Blackwell, 2000.

Engels, Friedrich. "Letter to the editor of the Northern Star, December 1, 1849." Online: http://www.marxists.org/archive/marx/works/1849/11/28.htm.

———. "The Communists and Karl Heinzen." *Deutsche-Brüsseler-Zeitung*, September-October 1847. Online: www.marxists.org/archive/marx/works/1847/09/26.htm.

Eriksen, Thomas Hylland. "Hvad du ser i Breivik siger mest om dig selv." *Information*, 25 April 2012.

Expo. *Den antimuslimska miljön. Idéerna, profilerna och begreppen*, 2011. Online: http://expo.se/www/download/den-antimuslimska-miljon-ideerna-profilerna-och-begreppen-SLUTVERSION1.2.pdf.

Fairclough, Norman. *Language and Globalization.* London: Routledge, 2006.

Ferraresi, Franco. *Threats to Democracy: The Radical Right in Italy after the War.* Princeton, NJ: Princeton University Press, 1996.

Fife, Graeme. *The Terror. The Shadow of the Guillotine, France 1792-1794.* London: Portrait, 2004.

Fine, Sidney. "Anarchism and the Assassination of McKinley." *American Historical Review* 60 (1955) 777–99.

Ford, Franklin. L. *Political Murder from Tyrannicide to Terrorism.* Cambridge, MA: Harvard University Press, 1985.

Ford, Henry. *My Philosophy of Industry*. London: George G. Harrap, 1929.

Forsthoff, Ernst. *Der Totale Staat*. Hamburg: Hanseatische Verlagsanstalt, 1930.

Foucault, Michel. *Society Must Be Defended*. London: Penguin, 2003 [1975/6].

———. *The Will to Knowledge*. London: Penguin, 1998 [1976].

Fraenkel, Ernst. *The Dual State. A Contribution to the Theory of Dictatorship*. New York: Octagon, 1969.

Freeden, Michael. *Ideologies and Political Theory: A Conceptual Approach*. Oxford: Clarendon, 1996.

Freedman, Lawrence. "The Third World War?." *Survival* 34 (2001) 61–88.

Freeman, Michael. "Democracy, Al Qaeda, and the Causes of Terrorism: A Strategic Analysis of U.S. Policy." *Studies in Conflict and Terrorism* 31 (2008) 40–59.

Friesen, Gerhard K., ed. *'Trotz alledem und alledem'. Ferdinand Freiligraths Briefe an Karl Heinzen 1845 bis 1848*. Bielefeld: Aisthesis, 1998.

Furet, Francois. "Terror." In *A Critical Dictionary of the French Revolution*, edited by Francois Furet and Mona Ozoud, 137–50. Cambridge, Mass., Belknap, 1989.

———, and Denis Richet. *La Révolution francaise*. Paris: Hachette, 1973.

Gardell, Mattias. "Antifeminism: Breivik's misogyny politically motivated." 4 June 2012. Online: http://feministisktperspektiv.se/2012/06/04/antifeminism-breiviks-misogyny-politically-motivated/.

———. "The roots of Breivik's ideology: where does the romantic warrior ideal come from today." 1 August 2011. Online: www.opendemocracy.net/print/60674.

Gaucher, Roland. *The Terrorists from Tsarist Russia to the OAS*. London: Secker & Warburg, 1965.

German General Staff. *War Book*. Mechanicsburg: Stackpole, 2005 [1902].

Gentile, Giovanni. "The Doctrine of Fascism," 1932. Online: www.worldfuturefund.org/wffmaster/reading/germany/mussolini.htm.

———. "Manifesto of the Fascist Intellectuals," 1925. Online: http://www.cmrs.ucla.edu/brian/research/unfinished/unfinished_books/manifesti.pdf.

———. "Origins and Doctrine of Fascism." in Giovanni Gentile, *Origins and Doctrine of Fascism: With Selections from Other Works*, 1–42. New Brunswick: Transaction, 2002 [1929].

———. "The Philosophic Basis of Fascism." *Foreign Affairs* 6 (1928) 290–304.

———. "What is Fascism?" In Giovanni Gentile, *Origins and Doctrine of Fascism: With Selections from Other Works*, 43–76. New Brunswick: Transaction, 2002 [1925].

Gershoy, Leo. *Bertrand Barere: A Reluctant Terrorist*. Princeton, NJ: Princeton University Press, 1962.

Goebbels, Joseph. "The Total Revolution of National Socialism." In *Fascism*, edited by Roger Griffin, 133–35, Oxford: Oxford University Press, 1995 [1939].

Gray, John. "Ever the twain. Review of Ian Buruma & Avishai Margalit: Occidentialism." *Times Literary Supplement* October 8 (2004) 25.

Gregory, Paul R. *Terror by Quota: State Security from Lenin to Stalin*. New Haven: Yale University Press, 2009.

Grob-Fitzgibbon, Benjamin. "From the dagger to the bomb: Karl Heinzen and the evolution of political terror." *Terrorism and Political Violence* 16 (2004) 97–115.

Grossrichard, Alain. *The Sultan's Court: European Fantasies of the East*. London: Verso, 1998.

Gunaratna, Rohan. "Terrorism in Southeast Asia – threat and response." In *The History of Terrorism from Antiquity to Al Qaeda*, edited by Gérard Chaliand and Arnaud Blin Berkeley, chapter 17. Berkeley, University of California Press, 2007.

Halliday, Fred. *The Middle East in International Relations. Power, Politics and Ideology.* Cambridge: Cambridge University Press, 2005.

Harrison, Alexander. *Challenging De Gaulle: The OAS and Counterrevolution in Algeria, 1954–1962.* New York: Praeger, 1989.

Harket, Håkon. "Kulturkatastrofen." *Weekendavisen*, 29 July 2011.

Harvey, A. D. "Johann Most in Prison – Three Unpublished Petitions." *Terrorism and Political Violence* 5 (1993) 336–45.

Haydon, Colin, and William Doyle, eds. *Robespierre.* Cambridge: Cambridge University Press, 1999.

Heinzen, Karl. *Communism and Socialism.* Indianapolis: Association for the Propagation of Radical Principles, 1881.

———. *Lessons of a Century: For the 4th of July, 1876.* Indianapolis: Association for the Propagation of Radical Principles, 1876.

———. "Murder." In *Voices of Terror*, edited by Walter Laqueur, 57–67. New York: Reed, 2004.

———. *Murder and Liberty.* Indianapolis: Association for the Propagation of Radical Principles, 1881.

———. *The True Character of Humboldt.* Indianapolis: Association for the Propagation of Radical Principles, 1869.

———. *What is Humanity?* Indianapolis: Association for the Propagation of Radical Principles, 1877.

———. *What is Real Democracy? Answered by an Exposition of the Constitution of the United States.* Indianapolis: Association for the Propagation of Radical Principles, 1871.

Hindess, Barry. "Liberalism—what's in a name?" In *Global Governmentality. Governing International Spaces*, edited by Wendy Larner and William Walters, 23–39. London: Routledge, 2004.

Hobbes, Thomas. *Behemoth.* London: Frank Cass, 1993 [1681].

———. *Leviathan.* London: Penguin, 1968 [1651].

Hobhouse, L.T. *Liberalism.* Oxford: Oxford University Press, 1964 [1911].

Holden, Barry. *Understanding Liberal Democracy.* Hertfordshire: Harvester Wheatsheaf, 1993.

Holmes, Stephen. *Passions and Constraint: On the Theory of Liberal Democracy.* Chicago: University of Chicago Press, 1995.

Honeck, Mischa. *We are the Revolutionists: German-speaking Immigrants and American Abolitionists after 1848.* Athens, Georgia: University of Georgia Press, 2011.

Huber, Hans. *Karl Heinzen. Seine politische Entwicklung und publizistische Wirksamkeit.* Bern: Paul Haupt, 1932.

International Crisis Group. "In their own words: reading the Iraqi insurgency." *Middle East Report* no. 50 (February 15, 2006).

Jackson, Richard. "The ghost of state terror: knowledge, politics and terrorism studies." *Critical Studies on Terrorism* 1 (2008) 377–92.

Jászi, Oscar., and John D. Lewis. *Against the Tyrant: The Tradition and Theory of Tyrannicide.* Glencoe: Free Press, 1957.

Jensen, Richard. B. "The International Campaign Against Anarchist Terrorism, 1880–1930s." *Terrorism and Political Violence* 21 (2009) 89–109.

Jentz, John B. "The 48ers and the Politics of the German Labor Movement in Chicago during the Civil War Era: Community Formation and the Rise of a Labor Press." In *The German-American Radical Press: The Shaping of a Left Political Culture, 1850–1940*, edited by Elliot Shore, Ken Fones-Wolf, and James P. Danky, 49–62. Urbana: University of Illinois Press, 1992.

Joas, Hans. *War and Modernity.* Cambridge: Polity, 2003.

Juergensmeyer, Mark. *Global Rebellion: Religious Challenges to the Secular State, From Christian Militias to Al Qaeda.* Berkeley: University of California Press, 2008.

———. *Terror in the Mind of God: The Global Rise of Religious Violence.* Berkeley: University of California Press, 2000.

Jünger, Ernst. "Die totale Mobilmachung." In *Krieg und Krieger*, 9–30. Berlin: Junker und Dünnhaupt, 1930.

Kahan, Alan S. *Aristocratic Liberalism: The Social and Political Thought of Jacob Burckhardt, John Stuart Mill and Alexis de Tocqueville.* Oxford: Oxford University Press, 1992.

Kant. Immanuel. "Streit der Fakultäteten." In *Kant Werke*, vol. 6, 261–393. Darmstadt: Wissenschaftliche Buchgesellschaft, 1966 [1798].

———. "Zum ewigen Frieden." In *Kant Werke*, vol. 6, 191–252. Darmstadt: Wissenschaftliche Buchgesellschaft, 1966.

Kaplan, Jeffrey. "Right Wing Violence in North America." *Terrorism and Political Violence* 7 (1995) 44–95.

———, and Heeléne Lööw, ed. *The Cultic Milieu. Oppositional Subcultures in an Age of Globalization.* Walnut Creek: Altamira, 2002.

———, and Tore Bjørgo, ed. *Nation and Race. The Developing Euro-American Racist Subculture.* Boston: Northeastern University Press, 1998

Kateb, Georg. *Hannah Arendt. Politics, Conscience, Evil.* Oxford: Martin Robertson, 1984.

Kates, Gary, ed. *The French Revolution. Recent debates and new controversies.* 2nd ed. London: Routledge, 2006.

Kennedy, Robert. "Is One Person's Terrorist Another's Freedom Fighter? Western and Islamic Approaches to 'Just War' Compared." *Terrorism and Political Violence* 11(1999) 1–21.

Kepel, Gilles. *The War for Muslim Minds. Islam and the West.* Cambridge, MA: Belknap, 2004.

Kershaw, Alister. *A History of the Guillotine.* London: John Calder, 1958.

Keynes, John Maynard Keynes. *The Economic Consequences of the Peace.* London: Macmillan, 1919.

Kirkpatrick, Jennett. *Uncivil Disobedience: Studies in Violence and Democratic Politics.* Princeton: Princeton University Press, 2008.

Kleber, John E. *The Encyclopedia of Louisville.* Louisville: University of Kentucky Press, 2001.

Koselleck, Reinhart. *Begriffsgeschichten. Studien zur Semantik und Pragmatik der politischen und sozialen Sprache.* Frankfurt am Main: Suhrkamp, 2006.

———. *Critique and Crisis: Enlightenment and the Pathogenesis of Modern Society.* Cambridge, MA: MIT Press, 1988.

———. "The Historical-Political Semantics of Asymmetric Counter-Concepts." In *Reinhart Koselleck, Futures Past*, 155–91. New York: Columbia University Press 2004.

Laqueur, Walter. *The Age of Terrorism*. London: Weidenfeld and Nicolson, 1987.

———. *The Political Psychology of Appeasement*. New Brunswick: Transaction, 1980.

———, and Yonah Alexander, eds. *The Terrorism Reader*, London: Penguin, 1991.

"The Law of 22 Prairial." *Telos* (2007) 92–100.

Le Bon, Gustave. *The Crowd. A Study of the Popular Mind*. New York: Dover Publications, 2002 [1895]

Lefebvre, Georges. *The Coming of the French Revolution*. Princeton: Princeton University Press, 2005 [1947].

Lefort, Claude. "The Revolutionary Terror." In *Democracy and Political Theory*, chapter 4. Cambridge: Polity, 1988.

Leiden, Carl and Karl M. Schmitt. *The Politics of Violence: Revolution in the Modern World*. Englewood Cliffs, NJ: Prentice-Hall, 1968.

Levine, Bruce. *The Spirit of 1848. German Immigrants, Labor Conflict, and the Coming of the Civil War*. Urbana: University of Illinois Press, 1992.

Lia, Brynjar. "Al-Qaida's Appeal: Understanding its Unique Selling Points." *Perspectives on Terrorism* 2 (2008) 3–10.

Lifton, Robert Jay. *The Nazi Doctors. Medical Killing and the Psychology of Genocide*. New York: Basic, 2000.

Locard, Henri. *Pol Pot's Little Red Book. The Sayings of Angkar*. Chiang Mai: Silkworm, 2004.

Locke, John. *Two Treaties of Government*. Cambridge: Cambridge University Press, 2004 [1690].

Ludendorff, Erich von. *Der totale Krieg*. Munich: Ludendorff, 1935.

Luttwak, Edward N. "Towards Post-Heroic Warfare." *Foreign Affairs* 74 (1995) 109–22.

Luzzatto, Sergio. "European Visions of the French Revolution." In *Revolution and the Meanings of Freedom in the Nineteenth Century*, edited by Isser Woloch, 31–64. Stanford, CA: Stanford University Press, 1996.

Macpherson, C. B. *The Life and Time of Liberal Democracy*. Oxford: Oxford University Press, 1977.

Mandela, Nelson. "I am prepared to die." 1964. Online: www.historyplace.com/speeches/mandela.htm.

Mann, Michael. "The autonomous power of the state: its origins, mechanisms and results." *Archives européennes de sociologie* 25 (1984) 185–213.

Marat, Jean-Paul. "The Execution of the Tyrant." *Journal de la République Francaise*. 23 January 1793. Online: http://www.marxists.org/history/france/revolution/marat/1793/tyrant.htm.

Marinetti, Filippo. "The Futurist Manifesto," 1909. Online: http://www.unknown.nu/futurism/manifesto.html.

Marx, Karl. "Moralising Criticism and Critical Morality. A contribution to German cultural history contra Karl Heinzen." *Deutsche-Brüsseler-Zeitung*, October-November 1847. Online: www.marxists.org/archive/marx/works/1847/10/31.htm.

Matzen, Jeppe. "Nyfascisten." *Weekendavisen*, 29 July 2011.

Mayer, Arno J. *The Furies: Violence and Terror in the French and Russian Revolutions*. Princeton, NJ: Princeton University Press, 2000.

McAuley, Denis. "The ideology of Osama bin Laden: Nation, tribe and world economy." *Journal of Political Ideologies* 10 (2005) 269–87.

McMahon, Darrin. *Enemies of the Enlightenment: The French Counter-Enlightenment and the Making of Modernity*. Oxford: Oxford University Press, 2001.

McVeigh, Timothy. "The McVeigh letters: Why I bombed Oklahoma." *The Observer*, 6 May 2001. Online: http://observer.guardian.co.uk/international/story/0,6903,486847,00. html.

Merkl, Peter H. *Political Violence and Terror: Motifs and Motivations*. Berkeley: University of California Press, 1986.

———, and Leonard Weinberg, ed. *Right-Wing Extremism in the Twenty-First Century*. London: Routledge, 2003.

Michael, George. *The Enemy of My Enemy: The Alarming Convergence of Militant Islam and the Extreme Right*. Kansas: University Press of Kansas, 2006.

———. "Michael Collins Piper: An American Far Right Emissary to the Islamic World." *Totalitarian Movements and Political Religions* 9 (2008) 61–78.

Michel, Lou and Dan Herbeck. *American Terrorist: Timothy McVeigh & the Oklahoma City Bombing*. New York: HarperCollins, 2001.

Michels, Robert. *Political Parties: A Sociological Study of the Oligarchic Tendencies of Modern Democracy*. New York: Free Press, 1962 [1911].

Mill, John Stuart. *Considerations on Representative Government*. In *Collected Works of John Stuart Mill*, vol. xix, 371–616. Toronto: University of Toronto Press, 1977 [1865].

———. *On Liberty*. In *Collected Works of John Stuart Mill*, vol. xviii, 213–310. Toronto: University of Toronto Press, 1977 [1859].

Miller, Martin. A. "The Intellectual Origins of Modern Terrorism in Europe." In *Terrorism in Context*, edited by Martha Crenshaw, 27–62. University Park: Pennsylvania State University Press, 1995.

Mosca, Gaetano. *The Ruling Elite*. New York: McGraw-Hill, 1939 [1923].

Musolff, Andreas. "Schreckenswörter an der Tagesordnung. Rezeptionen der Terreur-Terminologie der Französischen Revolution in Deutschland 1794–1800." in *Begriffsgeschichte und Diskursgeschichte*, edited by Dietrich et al., 187–209. Opladen: Westdeutscher Verlag, 1994.

Müller, Jan-Werner. *Contesting Democracy. Political Ideas in Twentieth-Century Europe*. New Haven: Yale University Press, 2011.

———. *A Dangerous Mind – Carl Schmitt in Post-War European Thought*. New Haven: Yale University Press, 2003.

Münkler, Herfried. *Politische Bilder, Politik der Metaphern*. Frankfurt: Fischer, 1994.

Nagler, Jorg. "The Lincoln-Fremont Debate and the Forty-Eighters." In *The German Forty-Eighters in the United States*, edited by Charlotte Brancaforte, 157–78. New York: Peter Lang, 1989.

Nietzsche, Friedrich. *Götzen-Dämmerung*. München: Wilhelm Goldmann, 1964.

Neocleous, Mark. "Long live death! Fascism, resurrection, immorality." *Journal of Political Ideologies* 10 (2005) 31–49.

———. "The Monstrous Multitude. Edmund Burke's Political Teratology." *Contemporary Political Theory* 3 (2004) 70–88.

Neue Deutsche Biographie. Vol. 8. Berlin: Duncker & Humblot, 1969.

New York Court of Special Sessions. "The People of the State of New York, Plaintiff, v. John Most, Defendant." 1901. Online: http://library.buffalo.edu/libraries/exhibits/panam/law/images/peoplevmost.html.

Nomad, Max. *Apostles of Revolution*. New York: Collier, 1961.

Olney, Richard. "The Development of International Law." *American Journal of International Law* 1 (1907) 418–30.

Ortega y Gasset, José. *The Revolt of the Masses*. New York: W.W. Norton, 1993 [1931].

Paine, Thomas. *The Rights of Man*. London: J. M. Dent, 1993 [1791].

Palmer, Robert R. *The Age of the Democratic Revolution: A Political History of Europe and America, 1760–1800, vol. 2: The Struggle*. Princeton, NJ: Princeton University Press, 1964.

Pape, Robert A. "The Strategic Logic of Suicide Terrorism." *American Political Science Review* 97 (2003) 1–19.

Pareto, Vilfredo. *The Rise and Fall of the Elites: An Application of Theoretical Sociology*. Totowa: Bedminister, 1968 [1901].

Pearce, Susanna. "Religious Sources of Violence." In *The Making of a Terrorist, vol. 3: Root Causes*, edited by James J.F. Forest, chapter 8. Westport, CT: Praeger, 2006.

Perdue, William D. *Terrorism and the State. A Critique of Domination Through Fear*. Westport, CT: Praeger, 1989.

Pilisuk, Marc, and Angela Wong. "State Terrorism: When the Perpetrator is a Government." In *The Psychology of Terrorism, vol. 1: Clinical Aspects and Responses*, edited by C. E. Stout, chapter 5. Westport, CT: Praeger, 2002.

Pion-Berlin, David. *The Ideology of State Terror. Economic Doctrine and Political Repression in Argentina and Peru*. Boulder: Lynne Rienner, 1989.

Pinker, Steven. "A History of Violence." *The New Republic*, March 19 2007.

Porter, Patrick. "Long wars and long telegrams: containing Al-Qaeda." *International Affairs* 85 (2009) 285–305.

Prasz, Line. "Malmö-skytten får livstidsdom," *Politiken*, 23 November 2012.

Preuss, Ulrich. K. "Constitutional Power-making for the new Polity." *Cardozo Law Review* 14 (1993) 636–60.

Qutb, Sayyid. *The Sayyid Qutb Reader. Selected Writings on Politics, Religion, and Society*, edited by Albert J. Bergesen. London: Routledge, 2008.

Rapoport, David C. *Assassination and Terrorism*. Toronto: Canadian Broadcasting Corporation, 1971.

———. "Fear and Trembling: Terrorism in Three Religious Traditions." *American Political Science Review* 78 (1984) 658–77.

———. "The Fourth Wave: September 11 in the History of Terrorism." *Current History* (2001) 419–35.

———. "Sacred terror: a contemporary example from Islam." In *Origins of Terror*, edited by Walter Reich, 103–30, Washington: Woodrow Wilson Center Press, 1998.

———, and Yonah Alexander, eds. *The Morality of Terrorism. Religious and Secular Justifications*. New York: Pergamon, 1982.

Rivera, José Antonio Primo de. "Total feeling." In *Fascism*, edited by Roger Griffin, 187–88, Oxford: Oxford University Press, 1995 [1934].

Rennie, Bryan, and Philip L. Tite, eds. *Religion, Terror and Violence. Religious studies perspectives*. London: Routledge, 2008.

Richet, Denis. "Coups d'état." In *A Critical Dictionary of the French Revolution*, edited by Francois Furet and Mona Ozoud, 11–19. Cambridge, Mass.: Belknap, 1989.

Richter, Melvin. "A Family of Political Concepts. Tyranny, Despotism, Bonapartism, Caesarism, Dictatorship 1750–1917." *European Journal of Political Theory* 4 (2005) 221–48.

Robespierre, Maximilien. "Opinion sur le jugement de Louis XVI, 3 December 1792." In *Oeuvres de Maximilien Robespierre*, vol. 9, 120–30. Paris: Presses Universitaires de France, 1967.

————. "Report on the Principles of Political Morality." In *The French Revolution*, edited by Paul H. Beik, 276–87. London: Macmillan, 1970 [1794].

Rousseau, Jean-Jacques. "State of War," in Rousseau, *The Social Compact and other later political writings*, 162–76. Cambridge: Cambridge University Press, 1997 [1750s].

Rubin, Barry, ed. *The Politics of Terrorism: Terror as a State and Revolutionary Strategy*, Washington, DC: John Hopkins University, 1989.

Savage, Rowan. "Disease Incarnate: Biopolitical Discourse and Genocidal Dehumanisation in the Age of Modernity." *Journal of Historical Sociology* 20 (2007) 404–40.

Scheffler, Thomas. "Apocalypticism, Innerworldly Eschatology, and Islamic Extremism." In *Religion und Gewalt: Japan, der Nahe Osten und Südasien*, edited by Ildikó Bellér-Hann and Lisette Gebhardt, 43–79. Halle: Orientwissenschaftliches Zentrum der Martin-Luther-Universität Halle-Wittenberg, 2003.

Schmitt, Carl. "Das Meer gegen das Land." In *Staat, Grossraum, Nomos*, 395–400. Berlin: Duncker & Humblot, 1995 [1941].

————. *Der Begriff des Politischen*. Berlin: Duncker & Humblot, 1996 [1932].

————. *Die Diktatur*. Berlin: Duncker & Humblot, 1994.

————. "Die Raumrevolution. Durch den totalen Krieg zu einem totalen Frieden." In *Staat, Grossraum, Nomos*, 388–94. Berlin: Duncker & Humblot, 1995 [1940].

————. *Geistesgeschichtliche Lage des heutigen Parlamentarismus*. München: Duncker & Humblot, 1926.

————. *Glossarium. Aufzeichungen der Jahre 1947–1951*. Berlin: Duncker & Humblot, 1991.

————. *Hamlet oder Hekuba. Der Einbruch der Zeit in das Spiel*. Stuttgart: Klett-Cotta, 1985 [1956].

————. *Hüter der Verfassung*. Berlin: Duncker & Humblot, 1996 [1931].

————. *Land und Meer*. Köln-Lövenich: Hohenheim, 1981 [1942].

————. "Machtpositionen des modernen Staates." In Schmitt, *Verfassungsrechtliche Aufsätze*, 367–71, Berlin: Duncker & Humblot, 2003 [1933].

————. *Politische Theologie*. München: Duncker & Humblot, 1934.

————. "Raum und Grossraum im Völkerrecht." In *Staat, Grossraum, Nomos*, 234–68. Berlin: Duncker & Humblot, 1995 [1940].

————. "Staat als ein konkreter, an eine geschichtliche Epoche gebundener Begriff." In *Verfassungsrechtliche Aufsätze aus den Jahren 1924–1954*, 375–85, Berlin: Duncker & Humblot, 2003 [1941].

————. "Staatliche Souveränität und freies Meer. Über den Gegensatz von Land und See im Völkerrecht der Neuzeit." In *Staat, Grossraum, Nomos*, 401–30. Berlin: Duncker & Humblot, 1995 [1941].

————. "Staatsethik und pluralistischer Staat." In Schmitt, *Positionen und Begriffe*, 151–65. Berlin: Duncker & Humblot, 1994 [1930].

————. "Strukturwandel des Internationalen Rechts." In *Frieden oder Pazifismus?*, 652–700. Berlin: Duncker & Humblot, 2005 [1943].

————. *Theorie des Partisanen. Zwischenbemerkung zum Begriff des Politischen*. Berlin: Duncker & Humblot, 2002 [1963].

————. "Totaler Feind, totaler Krieg, totaler Staat." In *Positionen und Begriffe*, 268–73, Berlin: Duncker & Humblot, 1994 [1937].

————. *Über die drei Arten des rechtswissenschaftlichen Denkens*. Hamburg: Hanseatische Verlagsanstalt, 1934.

————. "Weiterentwicklung des totalen Staats in Deutschland." In *Positionen und Begriffe*, 211–16. Berlin: Duncker & Humblot, 1994 [1933].

Scurr, Ruth. *Fatal Purity. Robespierre and the French Revolution*. London: Chatto & Windus, 2006.

Sedgwick, Mark. "Al-Qaeda and the Nature of Religious Terrorism." *Terrorism and Political Violence* 16 (2004) 795–814.

Seegmiller, Beau. "Radicalized Margins: Eric Rudolph and Religious Violence." *Terrorism and Political Violence* 19 (2007) 511–28.

Semelin, Jacques. *Purify and Destroy: The Political Uses of Massacre and Genocide*. London: Hurst, 2007.

Sieyès, Emmanuel. "What is the Third Estate." In *The French Revolution*, edited by Paul H. Beik, 16–36. London: Macmillan, 1970 [1789].

Skinner, Quentin. "Hobbes and the Purely Artificial Person of the State." *Journal of Political Philosophy* 7 (1999) 1–29.

————. *Liberty before Liberalism*. Cambridge: Cambridge University Press, 1998.

————. "Moral Principles and Social Change." In Skinner, *Visions of Politics, vol. I: Regarding Method*, 145–57. Cambridge: Cambridge University Press, 2002.

Slomp, Gabriella. "The Theory of the Partisan: Carl Schmitt's Neglected Legacy." *History of Political Thought* 26 (2005) 502–19.

Sluga, Hans. "The pluralism of the political: from Carl Schmitt to Hannah Arendt." *Telos* 142 (2008) 91–109.

Sluka, Jeffrey A., ed. *Death Squad. The Anthropology of State Terror*. Philadelphia: University of Philadelphia Press, 2000.

Smith, Philip. *Punishment and Culture*. Chicago: University of Chicago Press, 2008.

Soboul, Albert. *The French Revolution 1787–1799*. New York: Vintage, 1975.

————. *The Sans-Culottes: The Popular Movement and Revolutionary Government 1793–1794*. Princeton: Princeton University Press, 1980.

Socialdemokratiet. "Program for det danske Socialdemokrati." In *Danmark for folket*, 9–13. Copenhagen: Arbejdernes oplysningsforbund, 1936 [1913].

Sofsky, Wolfgang. *Violence. Terrorism, Genocide, War*. London: Granta, 2003.

Sontag, Susan. *Illness as Metaphor*. London: Penguin, 2002.

Sorel, Georges. *Reflections on Violence*. Mineola: Dover, 2004 [1919].

Spengler, Oswald. *Der Untergang des Abendlandes*. München: C.H. Beck, 1990 [1917].

Sprinzak, Ehud. "Right-Wing Terrorism in a Comparative Perspective: The Case of Split Delegitimization." In *Terror from the Extreme Right*, edited by Tore Bjørgo, 17–43. London: Frank Cass 1995.

Sproat, Peter A. "Can the state commit acts of terrorism? An opinion and some qualitative replies to a questionnaire." *Terrorism and Political Violence* 9 (1997) 117–50.

Stalin, Joseph. "Defects in Party Work and Measures for Liquidating Trotskyite and Other Double Dealers, March 3, 1937." Online: www.marxists.org/reference/archive/stalin/works/1937/03/03.htm.

Steiner, George. "Aspects of Counter-Revolution." In *The Permanent Revolution: The French Revolution and its Legacy 1789–1989*, edited by Geoffrey Best, 129–53. London: Fontana, 1988.

Steger, Manfred B. *The Rise of the Global Imaginary: Political Ideologies from the French Revolution to the Global War on Terror*. Oxford: Oxford University Press, 2008.

Stohl, Michael, and George A. Lopez, ed. *The State as Terrorist: The Dynamics of Governmental Violence and Repression*. Westport, CT: Greenwood, 1987.

Stout, Mark E., Jessica M. Huckabey, John R. Schindler, and Jim Lacey. *The Terrorist Perspectives Project: Strategic and Operational Views of al Qaida and Associated Movements.* Annapolis: Naval Institute Press, 2008.

Sutherland, Donald M. G. *France 1789-1815: Revolution and Counterrevolution.* Oxford: Oxford University Press, 1986.

Thewleit, Klaus. *Male Fantasies.* London: Polity, 1989.

Thornton, Thomas P. "Terror as a weapon of political agitation." In *Terrorism: Critical Concepts in Political Science,* edited by David C. Rapoport, 41-63. London: Routledge, 2006.

Thorup, Mikkel. "The Anarchist and the Partisan. Two Types of Terror in the History of Irregular Warfare." *Terrorism and Political Violence* 20 (2008) 333-55.

———. *Fornuftens perversion - modoplysning og 200 års krig imod fornuftens herredømme.* Aarhus: Aarhus University Press, 2008.

———. *An Intellectual History of Terror: War, Violence and the State.* London: Routledge 2010.

Tocqueville, Alexis de. *Democracy in America.* Chicago: University of Chicago Press, 2002 [1835/1840].

Tuchman, Arleen. "Only in a Republic Can it be Proved that Science has No Sex. Marie Elizabeth Zakrzewska (1829-1902) and the multiple meanings of science in the nineteenth-century United States." *Journal of Women's History* 11 (1999) 121-42.

Tugwell, Maurice A. J. "Guilt Transfer." In *Terrorism: Critical Concepts in Political Science, vol. 2: The Second or Anti-Colonial Wave,* edited by David C. Rapoport, 57-69. London: Routledge, 2006.

Tully, James. *An Approach to Political Philosophy: Locke in Contexts.* Cambridge: Cambridge University Press, 1993.

van den Heuvel, Geert. "Terreur, Terroriste, Terrorisme." In *Handbuch politisch-sozialer Grundbegriffe in Frankreich 1680-1820,* edited by Rolf Reichardt and Eberhard Schmitt, 89-132. München: R. Oldenbourg, 1985.

US Army. *Counterinsurgency,* FM 3-24, December 2006.

US Government. *National Security Strategy of the United States of America,* September 2002.

Wallerstein, Immanuel. *After Liberalism.* New York: New Press, 1995.

Walther, Rudolf. "Terror, Terrorismus." In *Geschichtliche Grundbegriffe,* edited by Reinhart Koselleck et al., 323-44. Stuttgart: Klett-Cotta, 1990.

Walzer, Michael. "Liberalism and the Art of Separation." Political Theory 12 (1984) 315-30.

———. *Regicide and Revolution: Speeches at the Trial of Louis XVI.* Cambridge: Cambridge University Press, 1974.

Weber, Max. "Parliament und Regierung im Neugeordneten Deutschland." In *Max Weber Gesamtausgabe,* vol. 15, edited by H. Baier et. al., 421-596. Tübingen: J. C. B. Mohr, 1984 [1918].

———. "Politics as Vocation." In *From Max Weber: Essays in Sociology,* edited by H.H. Gerth & C. Wright Mills, 77-128. London: Routledge 1991 [1919].

Weinberg, Leonard and Ami Pedahzur, eds. *Religious Fundamentalism and Political Extremism.* London: Frank Cass, 2004.

Westerlund, David, ed. *Questioning the Secular State: The Worldwide Resurgence of Religion in Politics.* London: Hurst & Company, 1996.

Wiktorowicz, Quintan. "A Genealogy of Radical Islam", *Studies in Conflict & Terrorism* 28 (2005) 75–97.

————, and John Kaltner. "Killing in the Name of Islam: Al-Qaeda's Justification for September 11." *Middle East Policy* 10 (2003) 76–92.

Wilkinson, Paul. *Terrorism versus Democracy: The Liberal State Response.* 2nd ed. London: Routledge, 2006.

Wittke, Carl. *Against the Current: The Life of Karl Heinzen.* Chicago: University of Chicago Press, 1945.

————. "Karl Heinzen's Literary Ambitions." *Monatshefte für deutschen Unterricht* 37 (1945) pp. 88–98.

————. *Refugees of Revolution: The German Forty-Eighters in America.* Philadelphia: University of Pennsylvania Press, 1952.

————. "The German Forty-Eighters in America: A Centennial Appraisal." *American Historical Review* 53 (1948) 711–25.

Wood, Ian S. *Crimes of Loyalty. A History of the UDA.* Edinburgh: Edinburgh University Press, 2006.

Wright, Joanne. *Terrorist Propaganda: The Red Army Faction and the Provisional IRA, 1968–86.* New York: St. Martin's, 1990.

Wright, Lawrence. *The Looming Tower. Al-Qaeda's Road to 9/11.* London: Penguin, 2007.

————. "The Rebellion Within. An Al Qaeda mastermind questions terrorism." *The New Yorker* (June 2, 2008).

Wright, Stuart A. "Strategic Framing of Racial-Nationalism in North America and Europe: An Analysis of a Burgeoning Transnational Network." *Terrorism and Political Violence* 21 (2009) 189–210.

Žižek, Slavoj. *The Year of Dreaming Dangerously.* New York: Verso, 2012.

Zulaika, Joseba, and William A. Douglass. *Terror and Taboo: The Follies, Fables and Faces of Terrorism.* London: Routledge, 1996.

* 9 7 8 1 6 2 5 6 4 8 9 8 3 *